This scholarly work delves into the intricate realm of megaprojects, characterized by their colossal scale, complexity, and societal impact. It offers a comprehensive analysis of the multifaceted challenges that confront these ventures, spanning stakeholder conflicts, environmental, social, and economic sustainability concerns, and the unique characteristics of each project. The book presents a structured exploration, spanning seven chapters, which combine theoretical frameworks and empirical insights. It elucidates the fundamental components essential for sustainable megaproject management, emphasizing the significance of social responsibility. It establishes a crucial link between critical infrastructure and sustainable development, unraveling paradoxes. Furthermore, it scrutinizes the state of research in the field, highlights critical areas in accounting studies within the context of megaprojects, and identifies emerging research trends. The book concludes by examining a specific case study of a transnational megaproject. In sum, this scientific endeavor aims to address the pressing challenges of sustainable megaproject management, providing a holistic and systemic approach that accounts for all dimensions of sustainability and inclusive stakeholder engagement. It contributes to the evolving discourse on the governance and management of transnational megaprojects in a dynamically changing world.

Dr. Dario Cottafava (Ph.D.) is a Researcher at the Department of Economics and Statistics of the University of Turin on hydrogen economy. Author of several scientific publications, his research interests span from social and environmental accounting to circular economy and the use of open data and new technologies for environmental sustainability. He is also a lecturer at the European Business School and GBSB Global in Barcelona.

Daniel Torchia (Ph.D.) is a Researcher at Bocconi University and Lecturer in Business Administration and Organizational Behavior at the University of Turin. Daniel specializes in qualitative methods and conducts critical research on different forms of organizations. He has published interdisciplinary research in top-ranked journals, including *Culture and Organization, The British Accounting Review, Business Strategy* and t*he Environment and Accounting, Auditing & Accountability Journal.*

Stefania Camoletto is a Postdoctoral Research Fellow in Economics at the University of Turin. Her research interests include local development studies, CSR, and social capital within local communities. Stefania complements more qualitative research methodologies and community studies collaborating with institutional bodies including the European Parliament's Research Office.

Dr. Laura Corazza is a Researcher and Lecturer at the Department of Management, University of Turin, and she is qualified as Associate Professor. Her research has been published in many books and peer-reviewed journals including *The British Accounting Review, Accounting, Auditing and Accountability Journal, Sustainability Accounting Policy and Management Journal*, and *Journal of Applied Accounting Research*. She is the co-Editor in Chief of the *Journal of Public Affairs.*

Sustainable management
of transnational megaprojects

Dario Cottafava, Daniel Torchia,
Stefania Camoletto, Laura Corazza

Sustainable management of transnational megaprojects

LONDON AND NEW YORK

G. Giappichelli Editore

First published 2024
by Routledge
4 Park Square, Milton Park, Abingdon, Oxon OX14 4RN

and by Routledge
605 Third Avenue, New York, NY 10158

Routledge is an imprint of the Taylor & Francis Group, an informa business

and by G. Giappichelli Editore
Via Po 21, Torino – Italia

© 2024 Dario Cottafava, Daniel Torchia, Stefania Camoletto, Laura Corazza

The right of Dario Cottafava, Daniel Torchia, Stefania Camoletto, Laura Corazza to be identified as authors of this work has been asserted in accordance with sections 77 and 78 of the Copyright, Designs and Patents Act 1988.

All rights reserved. No part of this book may be reprinted or reproduced or utilised in any form or by any electronic, mechanical, or other means, now known or hereafter invented, including photocopying and recording, or in any information storage or retrieval system, without permission in writing from the publishers.

Trademark notice: Product or corporate names may be trademarks or registered trademarks, and are used only for identification and explanation without intent to infringe.

British Library Cataloguing-in-Publication Data
A catalogue record for this book is available from the British Library

ISBN: 978-10-326-8559-5 (hbk-Routledge)
ISBN: 978-10-326-8561-8 (ebk-Routledge)
ISBN: 978-10-326-8560-1 (pbk-Routledge)
ISBN: 979-12-211-0472-1 (hbk-Giappichelli)

Typeset in Simoncini Garamond
by G. Giappichelli Editore, Turin, Italy

This book was funded by the Franco-Italian University (UIF/UFI), which awarded the research group with the UFI/UIF 2021 Prize for the project "Stakeholder management in bi-national mega-projects for sustainable development". We gratefully acknowledge the funding received, which made it possible to publish and print the book.

UNIVERSITÉ   UNIVERSITÀ
FRANCO   ITALO
ITALIENNE FRANCESE

The manuscript has been subjected to a peer review process prior to publication.

CONTENTS

	page
List of figures and tables	xi

Introduction

1.	Outline	1
2.	Motivation of research	2
3.	Aim of this book and research questions	4
4.	Summary	5
References		5

1. **Megaprojects and sustainable infrastructure: an historical overview**

1.1.	Megaprojects in a nutshell	7
	1.1.1. From individual to collective sublimes: toward the definition of a fifth sublime	9
1.2.	Sustainable infrastructure or infrastructural territorialization	10
1.3.	The need of a framework for sustainable infrastructure	13
1.4.	Toward a dialogic accounting approach	15
1.5.	Summary	16
References		17

2. **Towards sustainable development: megaproject social responsibility and stakeholder engagement**

2.1.	Introduction	21
2.2.	The social responsibilities of megaprojects	23
2.3.	Towards a relational stakeholder theory for megaproject management	24
2.4.	Managing stakeholders in megaprojects	27
2.5.	Summary	30
References		30

page

3. **Critical infrastructure and sustainable development: a paradoxical link**

    3.1. Introduction   37
    3.2. Defining critical infrastructure   38
    3.3. Mapping the research field on critical infrastructure sector and climate change   40
    3.4. Mapping the field on critical infrastructure and SDGs   42
    3.5. A benchmark analysis of critical infrastructural megaprojects in the transportation sector   44
        3.5.1. Methodology   45
        3.5.2. Impacts mentioned in the reports and connection to SDGs   46
    3.6. Summary   48
    3.7. Annex I: list of impacts   49
    References   52

4. **A literature review on impact accounting & stakeholder management**

    4.1. Main features of megaprojects   57
        4.1.1. Types of megaprojects   58
        4.1.2. Projects' phases   59
        4.1.3. Sustainable infrastructure's pillars   59
        4.1.4. Impact accounting category   60
    4.2. Methodology   61
        4.2.1. Research questions   62
        4.2.2. Protocol and research sample   62
        4.2.3. Coding framework   65
    4.3. Results   65
        4.3.1. Trend   66
        4.3.2. Journal   66
        4.3.3. Citation network   67
        4.3.4. Geographic distribution   68
        4.3.5. Topic trends   69
        4.3.6. Keyword co-occurrence   72
    4.4. Discussion   73
        4.4.1. Future research trends   76
    4.5. Summary   80
    References   81

page

5. **Environmental justice movement: social and environmental conflicts**

    5.1. The emergence of the environmental justice movement   91
        5.1.1. About free riders, commons and distributional economics   92
    5.2. Conflicts and megaprojects: the challenge of stakeholders' management   97
    5.3. Toward an inclusive and systemic management of infrastructure projects   100
    5.4. Summary   102
    References   102

6. **A historical and empirical analysis of stakeholders in the Turin-Lyon railway line: towards an inclusive and ecosystemic vision of stakeholder management**

    6.1. Introduction   107
    6.2. A short history of the Turin-Lyon high speed rail   108
    6.3. Methodology   113
    6.4. Results   114
    6.5. Summary   116
    References   116

7. **Between sustainability and social innovation: the importance of the local identity and communities**

    7.1. Introduction   119
    7.2. Background   120
        7.2.1. The crisis of the center periphery model: the complexity and new strategic centrality of mountain and metro-mountain areas   121
        7.2.2. A hybrid mountain: the case of the Susa Valley   123
        7.2.3. A new institutional perspective to overcome the "marginality" of places   126
    7.3. Methodology   127
    7.4. Results and findings   129
        7.4.1. A "responsible" ecosystem with a strong identity   133
    7.5. Conclusions   137
    7.6. Summary   139
    References   139

			page
8.	**Conclusion**		
	8.1.	A critique of the status quo	143
	8.2.	Limits and future opportunities	145
	8.3.	Summary	145
	References		146

Index   147

LIST OF FIGURES AND TABLES

page

Figure

Chapter two

Figure 1.	MSR framework	24

Chapter three

Figure 1.	Salient elements of Critical infrastructure	40
Figure 2.	Cartography of the megaprojects analyzed, representing critical infrastructure	44
Figure 3.	List of the SDGs most mentioned according to the SDG Mapper tool of the European Commission	47
Figure 4.	Specific SDGs sub-targets covered in our analysis	48

Chapter four

Figure 1.	Flowchart of the selection process for the considered contributions	65
Figure 2.	Number of contributions per year related to megaprojects and sustainable infrastructure in the business area	66
Figure 3.	Number of contributions per year for different sources (scientific journals and conferences)	67
Figure 4.	Co-citation network of scientific contributions for megaprojects and sustainable infrastructure in the business area	68
Figure 5.	Collaboration among countries and geographic distribution of scientific contributions related to megaprojects and sustainable infrastructure in the business area	69
Figure 6.	Cumulative occurrence of keywords from the selected corpus of literature	70

		page
Figure 7.	Wordcloud of top keywords within the corpus of literature	70
Figure 8.	Thematic evolution of top keywords from 1978 to 2022 of studies in the business area related to megaprojects and sustainable infrastructure	71
Figure 9.	Keyword co-occurrence network	72

Chapter seven

Figure 1.	Piedmont's valleys in dark gray and the research area including the Susa valley (1), the Sangone valley (2) and part of Chisone and Germanasca valleys (3)	125

Tables

Introduction

Table 1.	Research Questions	4

Chapter three

Table 1.	Main features of CI and climate change implications	42
Table 2.	Megaprojects used as a benchmark for the analysis of SDGs	46

Chapter four

Table 1.	Classification of the corpus of literature (only articles) into Topic, Type of infrastructure, Phase, Evaluation and Impact	73
Table 2.	Summary of future research trends per main topic area	79

Chapter seven

Table 1.	Interviewees	128

INTRODUCTION

ABSTRACT: *What is the role of management and accounting studies to shift from 'unsustainable' megaprojects to sustainable infrastructure and infrastructural megaprojects? What are the most recent research advancements to deal with the megaproject complexity, especially in transnational infrastructural projects? What are the best practices to manage transnational megaprojects with an inclusive and open approach? Starting from these research questions, and other sub-questions, this book aims to shed light on novel accounting and managerial practices to deal with the intrinsic complexity of megaprojects, including several aspects from stakeholder management and the impact of social conflicts on megaprojects costs to novel concepts and practices such as Megaprojects Social Responsibility and the need of geospatial socio-economic impact accounting framework.*

SUMMARY: 1. Outline. – 2. Motivation of research. – 3. Aim of this book and research questions. – 4. Summary. – *References.*

1. Outline

Megaprojects and large infrastructure represent the backbone of every developed society and Nation (Thacker et al., 2018). Megaprojects are typically defined as "*large-scale, complex ventures that typically cost US$1 billion or more, take many years to develop and build, involve multiple public and private stakeholders, are transformational, and impact millions of people*" (Flyvbjerg, 2014) including transportation infrastructure such as airport, high-speed railway (HSR), or maritime ports (Flyvbjerg et al., 2003), large hydroelectric power stations or dams (Stone, 2008), as well as political projects such as the Apollo programme (Horwitch, 1990) or temporary events as the Olympic Games (Golubchikov, 2017; Shakirova, 2015).

However, although their crucial role in shaping the society and support the economic and wealth development megaprojects' management still remain one of the so-called *wicked* problems, due to the high complexity caused by opposing stakeholder interests (Camargo & Vázquez-Maguirre, 2021), short versus long-term timespan, local versus national and international scale (Esposito et al., 2021), and many other complex technical aspects and social issues to be taken into account. In addition, the recent need to face with the current and urgent climate crisis moved the spotlight and questioned further on the sustainability – environmental, social and economic sustainability – of megaprojects and their role both in the short and in the long term toward a sustainable development (Corazza et al., 2022).

On top of these premises, this book is structured into 7 different chapters presenting both theoretical and empirical evidence on sustainable megaprojects and infrastructure. Specifically, it is divided as follows:

Chapter 1 briefly introduces the book by discussing fundamental concepts on sustainable infrastructure and megaprojects, and the related current managerial challenges.

Chapter 2 discusses the Megaproject Social Responsibility (MSR) framework and the need of engaging stakeholders (primary and secondary) from the earlier phases.

Chapter 3 presents the link between critical infrastructure and sustainable development.

Chapter 4 summarises the most recent scientific contributions on megaprojects and impact accounting by presenting the results of a systematic literature review.

Chapter 5 focuses on the social components of megaprojects management and its connection to the environmental justice concept by giving the most holistic view of megaprojects and related challenges and by discussing the need of adopting a system thinking approach for megaproject management.

Chapter 6 presents the case study, from a historical point of view, of the Turin-Lyon high-speed railway megaproject in Italy, object of the last chapters of this book. Moreover, it provides primary research on managers and directors of the public promoter of the project, TELT, to construct the stakeholder network from their perspective.

Chapter 7, finally, discusses the importance of the local territorial identity by focusing on the Susa Valley case study and the emergence of new forms of entrepreneurship in the Alpine Valley.

Chapter 8, concludes the book.

2. Motivation of research

Project Management is a complex issue and topic by definition. Megaproject and large infrastructure management is, hence, one of the so-called *wicked* challenges (Esposito & Terlizzi, 2023). Indeed, in the past decades, the management of large infrastructure, such as, for instance, high-speed railway lines (Esposito et al., 2021) and enormous renewable energy production plants (Li et al., 2013), has received a lot of attention to understand the underlying successful factors. According to the literature, for a successful management, all environmental, social, or economic positive/negative should be taken into account in the management from the earlier phase of the project (Wang & Pitsis, 2020), and a critical emphasis should be placed on managing stakeholder concerns using inclusive and open managerial strategies (Xue et al., 2022). Therefore, the use of specific accounting and monitoring techniques is required due to the difficulty of managing the many conflicting interests of the different stakeholders involved in a megaproject. On top of these considerations, the *'uniqueness bias'* (Flyvbjerg, 2014, p. 9), i.e., every megaproject is unique and different from all the others for technical, cultural, social, environmental or institutional aspects, makes megaproject management even more extreme and complex. It should be added that each megaproject has unique positive characteristics that could have a significant impact on how concerns of stakeholders are managed. For instance, the duration of the project or the region it affects, all have the potential to significantly influence the society and the environment. Moreover, the construction project at hand may take several decades to be completed, during which time the stakeholder group as a whole may change significantly. One merely needs to consider the political factors that frequently depend on local politics (central, regional, municipal) and administrations and that might affect the outcomes positively or negatively. Regarding geographic extension, it is important to keep in mind that megaprojects frequently involve transnational territories and may involve two or more neighbouring countries. The management of the economic and social construction implications in this particular situation is considerably affected by the policies of each state, providing even another layer of management complexity. The duration of construction work of mega-projects can be several decades, during which the composition of the stakeholders themselves can change considerably. One only has to think of the political influences that can shape constructive or obstructive decisions, and that very often depend on local politics and (central/regional/local) governments. In case the megaproject concerns two or more adjoining countries, usually the management of the economic and social construction impacts can be significantly affected by the policies of each state, adding a further level of management complexity. Last but not least, every megaproject insists on certain localities with place-based culture, tradition, social conditions, or project technical characteristics. Failure to consider these idiosyncrasies could lead to disagreements and opposition during the course of a megaproject.

For these, and many others, reasons, this book addresses the topic of (sustainable) megaproject management focusing on the case of transnational megaprojects and the inherent and corresponding managerial complexity.

3. Aim of this book and research questions

This book and research aims at providing and presenting theoretical insights and empirical evidence on the need to approach megaproject and large infrastructure management with a holistic and systemic view including all the three pillars of sustainability and an inclusive and open stakeholder management and governance. Each chapter presents a different point of view in megaproject management in order to give to the reader the most comprehensive vision of the wicked challenges that megaproject construction entails.

This work will address and try to answer a few main research questions and several sub-questions. First, three main questions frame the entire book:

1) What is the role of management and accounting studies to shift from 'unsustainable' megaproject to sustainable infrastructure?
2) What are the most recent research advancements to deal with the megaproject complexity, especially in transnational infrastructural projects?
3) What are the best practices to manage transnational megaprojects with an inclusive and open approach?

In addition, the following research questions will be discussed, one for each chapter of this book.

Table 1. Research Questions

Number	Research Questions
Chapter 1	1) What are the main components to be considered for a sustainable megaprojects management? 2) What are the main accounting frameworks for sustainable infrastructure?
Chapter 2	1) How do megaprojects, due to their complexity, costs and long-lasting impacts, have a duty of care and social responsibility?
Chapter 3	1) What relationship exists between critical infrastructure and sustainable development? 2) What paradoxes do critical infrastructure entail and why are they the solution but also a hindering factor to the social, environmental and economic problems to which they should contribute?

continued

Chapter 4	1) What are the main authors, journals and countries contributing to megaprojects and sustainable infrastructure projects in the business and accounting area? 2) What are the main research areas of accounting studies within the megaprojects and sustainable infrastructure field? 3) What are the current research gaps and future research trends for accounting studies toward the development of a sustainable infrastructure projects' management?
Chapter 5	1) What are the root causes of the iron law of megaprojects and the unavoidable delays in construction and operation? 2) How is the environmental justice movement intertwined with the development of megaprojects and infrastructure on a global scale?
Chapter 6	1) What is the socio-political path that has led the Turin-Lyon high-speed rail megaproject to become so contested in Italy, while being more accepted in France? 2) How do managers and directors of TELT conceive their network of stakeholders?
Chapter 7	1) What are the aspects that favour new entrepreneurial activities as well as the critical issues that hinder the establishment and development of new activities in mountain and metro-mountain areas? 2)How the local identity and some recent experiences such as that of the so-called 'new entrepreneurs-mountaineers' affect the local identity and the realisation of a megaproject?

Source: authors' own elaboration.

4. Summary

Hence, the book aims at filling the gap in current managerial practices for megaprojects due to the lack of holistic and systemic approaches able to integrate stakeholder management, impact accounting and/or project management. It presents and discusses the state-of-the-art of practices in business, management and accounting studies for the sustainable management of transnational megaprojects and large infrastructure, focusing on novel approaches such as the use of system thinking and/or inclusive stakeholder management processes and approaches.

References

Camargo, B.A. & Vázquez-Maguirre, M. (2021). Humanism, dignity and indigenous justice: the mayan train megaproject, Mexico. *Journal of Sustainable Tourism*, 29(2–3), 371–390.

Corazza, L., Cottafava, D. & Torchia, D. (2022). Toward Sustainable Infrastructural Megaprojects. In *SDGs in the European Region*. S.I. Publishing, 1–25.

Esposito, G., Nelson, T., Ferlie, E. & Crutzen, N. (2021). The institutional shaping of global megaprojects: The case of the Lyon-Turin high-speed railway. *International Journal of Project Management*, 39(6), 658–671.

Esposito, G. & Terlizzi, A. (2023). Governing wickedness in megaprojects: Discursive and institutional perspectives. *Policy and Society*, *42*(April), 131–147.

Flyvbjerg, B. (2014). What you should know about megaprojects and why: An overview. *Project Management Journal*, *45*(2), 6–19.

Flyvbjerg, B., Bruzelius, N. & Rothengatter, W. (2003). Megaprojects and Risk. In *Megaprojects and Risk*. Cambridge University Press.

Golubchikov, O. (2017). From a sports mega-event to a regional megaproject: the Sochi winter Olympics and the return of geography in state development priorities. *International Journal of Sport Policy*, *9*(2), 237–255.

Horwitch, M. (1990). From unitary to distributed objectives. The changing nature of major projects. *Technology in Society*, *12*(2), 173–195.

Li, K., Zhu, C., Wu, L. & Huang, L. (2013). Problems caused by the Three Gorges Dam construction in the Yangtze River basin: A review. *Environmental Reviews*, *21*(3), 127–135.

Shakirova, S. (2015). Country images of Kazakhstan: From stereotypes and critique to positive national branding. *Journal of Eastern European and Central Asian Research*, *2*(1). https://doi.org/10.15549/jeecar.v2i1.78.

Stone, R. (2008). Three Gorges Dam: Into the Unknown. *Science*, *321*(5889), 628–632.

Thacker, S., Adshead, D., Morgan, G., Crosskey, S., Bajpai, A., Ceppi, P., Hall, J. & O'Regan, N. (2018). *Underpinning Sustainable Development*. UNOPS.

Wang, A. & Pitsis, T. S. (2020). Identifying the antecedents of megaproject crises in China. *International Journal of Project Management*, *38*(6), 327–339.

Xue, J., Shen, G.Q., Deng, X., Ogungbile, A.J. & Chu, X. (2022). Evolution modeling of stakeholder performance on relationship management in the dynamic and complex environments of megaprojects. *Engineering, Construction and Architectural Management*.

Chapter 1

MEGAPROJECTS AND SUSTAINABLE INFRASTRUCTURE: AN HISTORICAL OVERVIEW

ABSTRACT: *This chapter introduces the most relevant concepts on the need of a framework for sustainable infrastructure and megaprojects discussing both empirical evidence and theoretical reflections, focusing especially on the social and institutional dimensions alongside the environmental and economic ones. As megaprojects and infrastructure represent the backbone of every developed society and nation, and due to the climate crisis, the transition toward sustainable infrastructure, as also promoted by the United Nations and the SDG 9 (Industry, Innovation and Infrastructure), is nowadays more urgent than ever. This first chapter, drawing on existing scientific and grey literature, provides the wider framework adopted in this book highlighting the urgency of including the social component, both in terms of engaged stakeholders and of infrastructure governance, in every future megaproject and infrastructural project.*

SUMMARY: 1.1. Megaprojects in a nutshell. – 1.1.1. From individual to collective sublimes: toward the definition of a fifth sublime. – 1.2. Sustainable infrastructure or infrastructural territorialization. – 1.3. The need of a framework for sustainable infrastructure. – 1.4. Toward a dialogic accounting approach. – 1.5. Summary. – *References.*

1.1. Megaprojects in a nutshell

Megaprojects are generally intended as "*large-scale, complex ventures that typically cost US$1 billion or more, take many years to develop and build, involve multiple public and private stakeholders, are transformational, and impact millions of people*" (Flyvbjerg, 2014, p. 6). Therefore, in other words, megaprojects are large – either in terms of budget, long lifespan and geographical area – projects with several impacts on the society and the environment. Despite the commonly used prefix Mega, strictly speaking, megaprojects should be defined as Giga or Tera projects due to their budget order of magnitude of billions of euros (mega refers to millions). Megaprojects include a wide array of infrastructural projects required by our society. These include transportation infrastructure such as airports, high-speed railway (HSR) and large train stations or harbors (Esposito et al., 2021), industrial and mining facilities (Brahm & Tarziján, 2015), temporary events such as the Olympic Games (Randeree, 2014; Shakirova, 2015; Sroka, 2021), energy facilities such as large renewable power plants (Stone, 2008) or large research centers such as the CERN (Krige, 1994) or ITER project (Coblentz, 2019). Infrastructure, either large or not, may be classified into networked or non-networked infrastructure (i.e. connected or non-interconnected with other infrastructure). Non-networked infrastructure includes all infrastructure that is not interconnected and necessary to other infrastructure (e.g. a house), while networked infrastructure includes that necessary to develop all the others (e.g. an energy power plants or a transportation hub). More specifically, non-networked infrastructure includes, among others, 1) housing and shelter, 2) healthcare centers, 3) schools, 4) markets, 5) industrial facilities, 6) community centers, 7) courts and prisons, 8) government buildings, while networked infrastructure refers to energy, transport, water, solid waste and digital communication facilities (Thacker et al., 2018).

Due to its crucial role for the (sustainable) development of every country in the world, in the last decades infrastructure experienced a huge increase in investment (Ma et al., 2020) and enormous investments are needed to build the necessary infrastructure to support national development. The OECD estimates that an average investment of around USD 6.9 trillion per year is required at the global level to support the development of adequate infrastructure before 2030 (to achieve the goals of the Agenda 2030) (NCE, 2016). In contrast, the current spending for infrastructure globally reaches USD 3.4 trillions per year, which is less than the 50% of what would be necessary to develop the required infrastructure to fulfil the Agenda 2030. To understand the scale of the phenomenon, the required investment before 2030 is more than USD 90 trillion, which is more than the total past investment and market value of all global infrastructure (OECD, 2019a). The order of magnitude of investments is clearly depicted, for instance, by the "*China-Pakistan Economic Corridor*" (CPEC). The CPEC is part of the global Chinese transportation strategy, the Belt and Road Initiative (Lu et al., 2018), which consists in the development of the new "*silk road*" that will connect China with the majority of the countries in the world through maritime and terrestrial pathways. To build the CPEC, the Pakistani part of the Belt and Road initiative, more than USD 60 billion will be necessary, which represents an amount larger than all of Pakistan's infrastructure investments until today (Thacker et al., 2019). Such an amount (i.e., USD 90 trillion) is therefore necessary either to renovate and replace old infrastructure and to build new one, especially in developing countries (around 60% of the total investment) which still need to develop and build its basic networked infrastructure (NCE, 2016).

Beyond the need to develop the minimum amount of required infrastructure, both to stimulate economic growth of countries and to achieve sustainable development according to the Agenda 2030, the reason to invest in megaprojects is not so straightforward. Indeed, in the past decades, megaprojects have been widely contested (Adityanandana & Gerber, 2019; Teo & Loosemore, 2010; van Marrewijk et al., 2016) for their huge negative environmental impacts, on local community and territory, for the sake of a better national or international, for instance, transportation or energy systems, *de facto* sacrificing the local common good and identity of territories and communities for a "superior" benefit.

Numerous examples, such as the social and environmental effects brought on by large-scale construction projects like the Three Gorges Dam (Li et al., 2013; Stone, 2008; Yang et al., 2007) or the Qinghai-Tibet Railway (Qiu, 2007), which have the potential to permanently alter the natural ecosystem and have an impact on the quality of life for millions of people, are well-known. The dam known as the Three Gorges is the largest hydroelectric power plant in the world. It was constructed across three valleys in China, forcing more than a million people to leave their homes. In addition to this, the dam had a number of detrimental environmental effects by permanently altering the natural ecosystem and resulting in a decline in water quality and a loss of biodiversity (Li et al., 2013). Inaugurated in 2006, the Qinghai-Tibet Railway (Qiu, 2007), instead, connects the interior of China with Lhasa, the capital of Tibet, and is the highest railway in the world (it exceeds 5,000 m above sea level). The project caused significant concern in the local and global communities since it was perceived as a neo-colonial infrastructure, rather than just a transportation infrastructure.

1.1.1. From individual to collective sublimes: toward the definition of a fifth sublime

Due to such social concerns and (eventual) negative environmental impacts (but not only), megaprojects, indeed, remain a high-risk investment both for private organizations and public institutions. If, on one side negative unavoidable impacts are one of the reasons for social protests and contestations, with consequent delay in the construction phase, on the other side, every megaproject is technically a very complex challenge and suffers of the so-called "*uniqueness bias*", as defined by Flyvbjerg (2014, p. 9). The uniqueness bias is the curse of megaprojects, as each megaproject is different from all others, in terms of either technical features, the social and cultural identity of the area involved, or environmental aspects. Contestations, technical difficulties and the intrinsic complexity, thus, in the past provoked constant and ever present delays, increase in costs and extremely prolonged public debates both in the academic (Corazza et al., 2023) and practitioner or policy-maker community (Debernardi et al., 2011). This needs holistic and systemic approaches to be managed (Shams Esfandabadi et al., 2023). Quoting Flyvbjerg (2017), every megaproject is affected by the "*iron law of megaproject*" (p. 11), i.e. the unavoidable delay in the realization, which ends in the "*over budget, over time, under benefits and over and over again*" law of megaprojects (around 90% of megaprojects end with delays and an increase in costs).

Hence, why do governments, policy- and decision-makers still invest billions of euros in megaprojects? The motivations lie in a purely individualistic and personalistic reason of primary stakeholders involved, rather than in the interests of secondary ones, i.e. as stated by Flyvbjerg (2014) the *four sublimes*. Despite the great and undoubted difficulties and negative effects, practitioners and policy-makers are still excited and attracted by creating and developing unique projects in terms of technical difficulties (technological sublime), aesthetical appearance (aesthetic sublime), social and political impacts (political sublime) or economic benefit (economic sublime). Indeed, engineers, designers/architects, policy-makers or managers are always attracted by one of such sublimes and achievements. The search for the sublime, drawing on the definition of Kant of "absolute great", i.e. "greatness that is equal only to itself", is not new and is a common unavoidable human desire, well-known and analyzed in philosophy and arts. Therefore, the concrete challenge related to megaprojects and infrastructure is not on how to avoid such human ambition, but rather on how to manage and shift such individual ambition toward a collective one, and to shift the construction industry from megaprojects to sustainable infrastructure, aiming at regenerating local ecosystems. In this sense, what is missing from the description of Flyvbjerg (2014) is a fifth sublime, the willingness to positively impact and regenerate the world (partly included in the political sublime), to integrate the artificial world with the natural one, according to a posthuman vision where humans are only part of a larger ecosystem (Braidotti, 2019), where the individualistic and anthropocentric sublimes are replaced by a set of "*ecosystem sublimes*", shifting from the individual sublimes toward new (still to be defined) collective (Williams, 2013) and democratic (Frank, 2021) sublimes.

1.2. Sustainable infrastructure or infrastructural territorialization

Infrastructure systems are responsible for 60% of the world's GHG emissions (OECD, 2019). Planning for sustainable infrastructure is therefore essential to achieving sustainable development and meeting the Agenda 2030 objectives. According to Bhattacharya et al. (2019), infrastructure systems encompass both natural (such as land, forests, and oceans) and manmade (such as energy, water, and waste management systems, transportation, and telecommunications) systems. The Inter-American Development Bank (2018) states that sustainable infrastructure should not just be used as a synonym for green infrastructure (such as a renewable energy power plant) but are defined as *"infrastructure projects that are planned, designed, constructed, operated, and decommissioned in a manner to ensure economic and financial, social, environmental (including climate resilience), and institutional sustainability over the entire life cycle of the project"* (p. 11). Therefore, during the design, operating, and dismantling phases of a sustainable infrastructure, the project complexity – in terms of life duration, created impacts, and affected stakeholders – must be taken into account (OECD, 2019b).

A nation's wealth can be increased through sustainable infrastructure planning in a number of ways that are directly related to the SDGs, including by enhancing health and well-being (SDG 3), ensuring access to clean energy (SDG 7), promoting sustainable industrialization (SDG 9) and urban environments (SDG 11). In addition, by enhancing and enabling transportation networks and people's mobility, sustainable infrastructure may conserve marine (SDG 14) and terrestrial (SDG 15) environments as well as reducing inequality (SDG 10). The 17 SDGs are divided into three concentric circles: wellbeing, infrastructure, and natural environment. The infrastructure subset (SDGs 2, 6, 7, 8, 9, 11 and 12) serves as an enabler and a bridge to promote well-being (SDGs 1, 3, 4, 5, 10, 16) while maintaining the natural environment (SDGs 13, 14, 15). Waage et al. (2015) proposed this simple framework to better frame the relationships between the SDGs and sustainable infrastructure. The first-level objectives, then, are those people-centered and concerned with people's health, poverty, education, gender equality, and the advancement of an inclusive society. The second-level objectives (the infrastructure layer) are required to accomplish these aims. Therefore, sustainable infrastructure is essential to enhancing the production and distribution of products and commodities required to sustain people's well-being (first-level goals) in the areas of energy, clean water, food, transportation, and in general urban contexts, while avoiding negative impacts on the natural environment, which is reflected by the third-level goals linked to climate change, biodiversity preservation, and land and ocean conservation.

More specifically, although the aforementioned goals may be thought of as the core subset of infrastructure-related SDGs, infrastructure development does not solely refer to them. Indeed, because they form the foundation of society, infrastructure systems have an impact on numerous objectives, both positively and negatively. 72% of targets are directly or indirectly influenced by infrastructure, according to Thacker et al.'s (2019) analysis. This finding highlights the need for policymakers to adopt long-term visions and planning strategies to achieve national sustainable development by avoiding silos and field-specific analyses and decisions. The strategy and the vision behind the decision to move forward with a large infrastructure are even more important than the management of the planning, construction, and operation phases of a megaproject, because megaprojects present the opportunity to reduce space and increase economic interchanges (e.g., transportation infrastructure), to increase local or national wealth (industrial facilities), as well as to benefit the environment (transport or energy infrastructure). By boosting the productivity of the current industrial sectors, megaprojects are the fundamental framework that enables lowering the cost of transportation and energy production. Therefore, the size of megaprojects has the potential to have a long-term impact on entire regions or entire countries, either positively or badly, by profoundly altering not just the immediate environment but also the social and economic circumstances of the local population (Flyvbjerg et al., 2003).

Megaprojects and the associated construction work take decades to be completed. Likewise with the accompanying effects they cause or can prevent. Failures or poorly designed infrastructure could, in this sense, force vast regions to pursue unsustainable development for years (OECD, 2019b). For instance, megaprojects and mega-infrastructure played a key role in colonial activities in developing nations throughout the previous century and were the cause of what is referred to as "*infrastructural territorialization*" (Lesutis, 2021). Territorialization of the infrastructure is the situation in which the development and creation of "territoriality" are a result of the infrastructure itself. For instance, in Kenya, the Uganda Railway had an unpredictable and unplanned influence on the region. In fact, a large concentration of Europeans was brought on by the Uganda Railway in the early part of the 20th century, which prompted the development of new urban centers along a 10-km stretch of land (Jedwab et al., 2017). Nairobi, which was merely a small area at the beginning of the 20th century, was selected as a construction station for the railroad, which led to its rapid growth (Lesutis, 2021). Similarly, large transportation infrastructure may influence indigenous communities, as the Mayan train megaproject in Mexico (Camargo & Vázquez-Maguirre, 2021) or entire cities and urban areas such as the Olympic games in Barcelona in Spain (Chappelet, 2014; C. Kennett & De Moragas, 2006) that shaped the city landscape and entire neighbourhoods. Therefore, it is clear that the role of megaprojects is beyond the simple societal benefits generated by the provided services (e.g. energy produced, transport of people) – benefits that can be also provided, in a smaller scale, by generic infrastructure (not megaprojects) by reducing eventual negative impacts. Recalling the ideas of the four sublimes (Flyvbjerg, 2014), it is now clear the necessary shift from individualistic sublimes to collective ones, including long-term impacts and the "territorialisation" effect of megaprojects that goes far beyond mere accounting approaches or stakeholder engagement processes.

1.3. The need of a framework for sustainable infrastructure

Academic institutions and international organizations have worked together over the past years to develop general frameworks that might help to grasp all the ramifications that the building and maintenance of large infrastructure may have. For example, building on the well-known 3E framework of environment, economy, and equity, the UN Commission for Sustainable Development proposed four macro-areas in 2001 (United Nations, 2001) toward a framework for sustainability that includes indicators for people's health, education, and security as well as for the preservation of the land, the seas, and biodiversity. Other organizations, like the World Bank or the Group of Seven (G7), put more emphasis on the financial and governance components. In order to promote quality infrastructure investment, the G7 group, for instance, signed a self-commitment containing five principles: 1) ensuring effective governance; 2) ensuring job creation; 3) addressing social and environmental impacts; 4) ensuring alignment with economic and development strategies; and 5) enhancing effective resource mobilization (G7, 2016). With the help of these principles, the discussion of the governance model for sustainable infrastructure was highlighted, paying particular attention to the function of public-private partnerships in facilitating investments. Additionally, the Inter-American Development Bank (2018) suggested a novel framework with 14 aspects (including, for example, poverty, social impact, human and labour rights), more than 60 specific criteria, and was based on the four relevant dimensions – *economic, social, environmental, and institutional* – previously identified by other institutions. The governance at the local, national, and international levels (such as *Global and National Strategies*) as well as the importance of accounting and management systems for sustainable infrastructure are highlighted in the suggested framework. The institutional component encompasses elements like *global and national strategies, systemic change and gov-*

ernance, *management systems and accountability*, and *capacity building*; as a result, it also highlights the necessity of management systems and accountability for transparent governance.

In this sense, it is particularly noteworthy and innovative the fourth component, i.e. *institutional sustainability*. Indeed, institutional sustainability implies that, alongside the well-known and debated three E and the accounting and management of the social, environmental and economic impacts, it is crucial to adopt inclusive, transparent and open governance. Hence, according to institutional sustainability, new investments in sustainable infrastructure must be in line with the global agenda and the creation of national policies (United Nations, 2015). To support decision-makers during the planning, construction, and operation phases as well as to ensure transparency and boost confidence in the involved institutions, whether public or private, data collection and monitoring tools, assessment, and evaluation approaches are essential. The lack of information on contracts between the government and contractors, or between the main contractor and subcontractors, and more generally the lack of transparency in the management, tends to raise concerns in the civil society about potential bribery, fraud, and corruption since megaprojects and sustainable infrastructure are considered to be public goods (OECD, 2016). In that regard, the Organization for Economic Development (OECD) acknowledged that "*Infrastructure is primarily a governance challenge*" and listed ten major obstacles to manage infrastructure, ranging from the creation of a strategic vision (challenge 1) to the control of threats, to integrity (challenge 2) to the release and disclosure of useful data (challenge 8), to the resilience of the infrastructure (challenge 10). Bribery and corruption are particularly common (Flyvbjerg et al., 2003) in megaprojects and according to the Construction Sector Transparency Initiative, between 10% and 30% of infrastructure projects with public funding are lost to corruption. Four key industries – extraction and mining, building and construction, transportation, and ICT infrastructure – accounted for over 60% of these incidents (OECD, 2016).

The application of evidence-based instruments, including ex-ante and ex post impact assessments and reporting standard, should be mandatory to address this issue in order to prevent controversies and actively involve all key stakeholders throughout all phases of an infrastructure's lifecycle. Because of the "*uniqueness bias*" (Flyvbjerg, 2014, p. 9), there is no *one-size-fits-all* instrument for infrastructure auditing; instead, the right tools should be carefully chosen while taking into account the unique characteristics of the analyzed infrastructure and the impacted area. Decision-makers typically use cost-benefit analyses (CBAs) or environmental and social impact assessments (ESIAs), although the social component is frequently ignored (Khan, 2020; Mottee et al., 2020).

Concluding, it is not easy to choose the right tool. For example, categorization of tools and instruments may be done according to the project's lifecycle stage – 1. Prioritisation, 2. Planning/Preparation, 3. Procurement, 4. Detailed Design, 5. Finance, 6. Construction, and 7. Operation/Maintenance – and the corresponding infrastructure sector – general, transport, and energy (OECD, 2019b). Similarly, OECD (2018) divided the available norms and tools into three major groups in a different report: 1) Policy-related tools and instruments, 2) Project-related tools and instruments, and 3) Infrastructure-related data. Among others, Policy-related tools include a long list of instruments categorized in Framework, Financing, Governance, Development and Environment, while the Project-related tools are classified according to the different phases of a (Mega) project or infrastructure such as Planning and Prioritization, Institutional Capacity for Project Development, Project Preparation, and Transaction Support and Contract Management. Concluding, the Sustainable Infrastructure Tool Navigator (German Cooperation and UNEP, 2022), a web platform created by German Cooperation (implemented by the GIZ) in cooperation with the UNEP (United Nations Environment Programme) and the Sustainable Infrastructure Partnership (SIP), currently offers the most complete collection of tools, standards, and instruments (more than 50 instruments have been collected).

1.4. Toward a dialogic accounting approach

From this first chapter on sustainable infrastructure and the challenge of megaproject management, it is now clear that accounting and managerial studies should not simply focus on the management of the impacts or on the technical side of project management but on the institutional components of the most recent framework for sustainable infrastructure. Hence, a shift toward *Dialogic Accounting* (DA) practices, rather than *Monologic Accounting* is nowadays necessary. To recognize the role of stakeholders in organizations and to comprehend and decipher the mechanisms by which non-governmental organizations (NGOs), citizens, local communities, and the general civil society influence an organization's strategies and actions, dialogic accounting has become increasingly important in recent decades (Manetti et al., 2021). Stakeholders should be included in decision-making processes because they can lead an organization to shared solutions and shared values through their dialogic behaviours (Bellucci et al., 2019), if and only if the multidimensionality of interactions and conversations with and among stakeholders is acknowledged (O'Dwyer, 2005). DA has its origins in the groundbreaking research of the sociologist Habermas (1985), the political scientist Chantal Mouffe (1999, 2011), and the educator and philosopher Paulo Freire (1970). Habermas distinguishes between communicative and instrumental/strategic activities as two different categories of actions. The former seeks to achieve consensus and ensure that everyone participating in the discussion is aligned; the latter, however, is more concerned with achieving practical success.

In conclusion, dialogical accounting theory must be the foundation for sustainable infrastructure as well as megaproject planning and management because the impacts and consequences of infrastructure will affect a wide range of stakeholders, many of whom have conflicting interests. Furthermore, the disagreement between opposing visions and worries may be made worse by the high level of uncertainty in long-term future scenarios. Indeed, there may be a conflict between private and public interests. For instance, as businesses, contractors, and governments work to create infrastructure to benefit the entire population and community or their own economic interests, local residents and landowners fight to safeguard their properties and legal rights. Conflicts may also arise when combining short- and long-term goals. While politicians seek to create short-term job opportunities in order to achieve political consensus, environmentalists may want to protect and preserve natural ecosystems (although one of the most frequently advanced arguments is that benefits from infrastructure in the long-term may be notable and not negligible at local and global scales). In the next chapters of the book, dialogic accounting practices will be discussed in more detail by providing empirical evidence of the needs of a democratic and inclusive stakeholder management process and concrete examples and case studies.

1.5. Summary

This chapter introduces the main topics of megaprojects and sustainable infrastructure by framing the fundamental concepts necessary to face the complexity of megaprojects and large infrastructure. Starting from the *iron law*, the *uniqueness bias* and the *four sublimes*, concepts introduced by Flyvbjerg, the discussion then focused on the need of a framework for sustainable infrastructure. Specifically, according to the Inter-American Development Bank (2018) four relevant dimensions need to be considered for every sustainable infrastructure, namely, economic, social, environmental and institutional. From the social and institutional components, in particular, emerged the necessity to introduce a dialogic accounting approach, instead of a monologic one, to include all affected and involved stakeholders and to develop a democratic and inclusive stakeholder management process during every phase of a megaproject, from the planning to the construction or the operation phase.

References

Adityanandana, M. & Gerber, J.-F. (2019). Post-growth in the Tropics? Contestations over Tri Hita Karana and a tourism megaproject in Bali. *Journal of Sustainable Tourism*, 27(12), 1839–1856.

Bellucci, M., Simoni, L., Acuti, D. & Manetti, G. (2019). Stakeholder engagement and dialogic accounting: Empirical evidence in sustainability reporting. *Accounting, Auditing and Accountability Journal*, 32(5), 1467–1499.

Bhattacharya, A., Contreras Casado, C., Jeong, M., Amin, A.-L., Watkins, G. & Zuniga, M.S. (2019). *Climate Change Division Attributes and Framework for Sustainable Infrastructure Consultation Report*. http://www.iadb.org.

Brahm, F. & Tarziján, J. (2015). Does complexity and prior interactions affect project procurement? Evidence from mining mega-projects. *International Journal of Project Management*, 33(8), 1851–1862.

Braidotti, R. (2019). *Posthuman knowledge*. Polity Press.

Camargo, B.A. & Vázquez-Maguirre, M. (2021). Humanism, dignity and indigenous justice: the mayan train megaproject, Mexico. *Journal of Sustainable Tourism*, 29(2–3), 371–390.

Chappelet, J.L. (2014). Managing the size of the Olympic Games. *Sport in Society*, 17(5), 581–592.

Coblentz, L. (2019). Megaprojects: 1 ITER: Moving Towards Industrial-scale Fusion. *Resonance*, 1111–1123.

Corazza, L., Torchia, D. & Cottafava, D. (2023). Academics Applying Interventionist Research to Deal with Wicked and Complex Societal Problems. *Social and Environmental Accountability Journal*, (6), 1–18.

Debernardi, A., Grimaldi, R. & Beria, P. (2011). Cost-benefit analysis to assess modular investment: the case of the New Turin-Lyon Railway. *Contemporary Issues in CBA in the Transport Sector*, 1–15.

Esposito, G., Nelson, T., Ferlie, E. & Crutzen, N. (2021). The institutional shaping of global megaprojects: The case of the Lyon-Turin high-speed railway. *International Journal of Project Management*, 39(6), 658–671.

Flyvbjerg, B. (2014). What you should know about megaprojects and why: An overview. *Project Management Journal*, 45(2), 6–19.

Flyvbjerg, B. (2017). Introduction: The Iron Law of Megaproject Manage-

ment. In *The Oxford Handbook of Megaproject Management*. Oxford University Press, 1–18.
Flyvbjerg, B., Bruzelius, N. & Rothengatter, W. (2003). Megaprojects and Risk. In *Megaprojects and Risk*. Cambridge University Press.
Frank, J. (2021). *The Democratic Sublime: On Aesthetics and Popular Assembly*. Oxford University Press.
Freire, P. (1970). *Pedagogy of the oppressed*. The Continuum International Publishing Group Inc.
G7 (2016). *G7 Ise-Shima Principles for Promoting Quality Infrastructure Investment*. https://sustainable-infrastructure-tools.org/tools/g7-ise-shima-principles-for-promoting-quality-infrastructure-investment/.
German Cooperation and UNEP. (2022). *Sustainable Infrastructure Tool Navigator*. https://sustainable-infrastructure-tools.org/.
Habermas, J. (1985). *The theory of communicative action: Volume 1: Reason and the rationalization of society*. Beacon Press.
Inter-American Development Bank (2018). *What is Sustainable Infrastructure? A Framework to Guide Sustainability Across the Project Cycle*.
Jedwab, R., Kerby, E. & Moradi, A. (2017). History, Path Dependence and Development: Evidence from Colonial Railways, Settlers and Cities in Kenya. *The Economic Journal*, 127, 1467–1494.
Kennett, C. & De Moragas, M. (2006). Barcelona 1992: evaluating the Olympic legacy. In *National identity and global sports events: Culture, politics, and spectacle in the Olympics and the football World Cup*. State University of New York Press, 177–195.
Khan, I. (2020). Critiquing social impact assessments: Ornamentation or reality in the Bangladeshi electricity infrastructure sector? *Energy Research and Social Science*, 60(February), 101339.
Krige, J. (1994). Megaprojects, megateams and motivation. *Physics World*, 7(5), 17–18.
Lesutis, G. (2021). Infrastructural territorialisations: Mega-infrastructures and the (re)making of Kenya. *Political Geography*, 90(October), 102459.
Li, K., Zhu, C., Wu, L. & Huang, L. (2013). Problems caused by the Three Gorges Dam construction in the Yangtze River basin: A review. *Environmental Reviews*, 21(3), 127–135.
Lu, H., Rohr, C., Hafner, M. & Knack, A. (2018). *China Belt and Road Initiative: Measuring the impact of improving transportation connectivity on trade in the region*. RAND Corporation.
Ma, H., Liu, Z., Zeng, S., Lin, H. & Tam, V.W.Y. (2020). Does megaproject social responsibility improve the sustainability of the construction industry? *Engineering, Construction and Architectural Management*, 27(4), 975–996.

Manetti, G., Bellucci, M. & Oliva, S. (2021). Unpacking dialogic accounting: a systematic literature review and research agenda. *Accounting, Auditing & Accountability Journal*, 34(9), 250–283.

Mottee, L.K., Arts, J., Vanclay, F., Miller, F. & Howitt, R. (2020). Metro infrastructure planning in Amsterdam: how are social issues managed in the absence of environmental and social impact assessment? *Impact Assessment and Project Appraisal*, 38(4), 320–335.

Mouffe, C. (1999). Deliberative Democracy or Agonistic Pluralism? *Social Research*, 66(3), 745–758.

Mouffe, C. (2011). On the political. In *On the Political,* Routledge, 1–154.

NCE (2016). *The sustainable infrastructure imperative: financing for better growth and development.* New Climate Economy. http://newclimateeconomy.report/2016/wp-content/uploads/sites/4/2014/08/NCE_2016 Report.pdf.

O'Dwyer, B. (2005). Stakeholder democracy: challenges and contributions from social accounting. *Business Ethics: A European Review*, 14(1), 28–41.

OECD (2016). *Getting Infrastructure Right: The Ten Key Governance Challenges and Policy Options.*

OECD (2018). *G20/OECD/WB Stocktake of Tools and Instruments Related to Infrastructure as an Asset Class-Background report*, (July).

OECD (2019a). *Sustainable Infrastructure for Low-Carbon Development in Central Asia and the Caucasus.*

OECD (2019b). *Sustainable Infrastructure for Low-Carbon Development in Central Asia and the Caucasus Hotspot Analysis and Needs Assessment.*

Qiu, J. (2007). Life on the roof of the world. *Nature*, 449(27).

Randeree, K. (2014). Reputation and mega-project management: Lessons from host cities of the olympic games. *Change Management*, 13(2), 1–7.

Shakirova, S. (2015). Country images of Kazakhstan: From stereotypes and critique to positive national branding. *Journal of Eastern European and Central Asian Research*, 2(1).

Shams Esfandabadi, Z., Cottafava, D., Corazza, L. & Scagnelli, S.D. (2023). Sustainability Challenges of High-speed Railway Megaprojects from a Systems Thinking Lens. *Complexity and Sustainability in Megaprojects*, (June).

Sroka, R. (2021). Mega-projects and mega-events: evaluating Vancouver 2010 stadium and convention infrastructure. *Journal of Sport and Tourism*, 25(3), 183–200.

Stone, R. (2008). Three Gorges Dam: Into the Unknown. *Science*, 321(5889), 628–632.

Teo, M.M.M. & Loosemore, M. (2010). Community-based protest against construction projects: The social determinants of protest movement continuity. *International Journal of Managing Projects in Business*, 3(2), 216–235.

Thacker, S., Adshead, D., Morgan, G., Crosskey, S., Bajpai, A., Ceppi, P., Hall, J. & O'Regan, N. (2018). *Underpinning Sustainable Development.* UNOPS.

Thacker, S., Adshead, D., Fay, M., Hallegatte, S., Harvey, M., Meller, H., O'Regan, N., Rozenberg, J., Watkins, G. & Hall, J.W. (2019). Infrastructure for sustainable development. *Nature Sustainability*, 2(4), 324–331.

United Nations (2001). *Indicators of Sustainable Development: Framework and Methodologies.* Background Paper No. 3.

United Nations (2015). *The Sustainable Development Agenda.* https://www.un.org/sustainabledevelopment/development-agenda/.

van Marrewijk, A., Ybema, S., Smits, K., Clegg, S. & Pitsis, T. (2016). Clash of the Titans: Temporal Organizing and Collaborative Dynamics in the Panama Canal Megaproject. *Organization Studies*, 37(12), 1745–1769.

Waage, J., Yap, C., Bell, S., Levy, C., Mace, G., Pegram, T., Unterhalter, E., Dasandi, N., Hudson, D., Kock, R., Mayhew, S., Marx, C. & Poole, N. (2015). Governing the UN sustainable development goals: Interactions, infrastructures, and institutions. *The Lancet Global Health*, 3(5), e251–e252.

Williams, H. (2013). The Oswald Review: An International Journal of Undergraduate Research and Criticism in the Discipline of English. *An International Journal of Undergraduate Research and Criticism in the Discipline of English*, 15. https://scholarcommons.sc.edu/cgi/viewcontent.cgi?article=1136&context=tor.

Yang, S.L., Zhang, J. & Xu, X.J. (2007). Influence of the Three Gorges Dam on downstream delivery of sediment and its environmental implications, Yangtze River. *Geophysical Research Letters*, 34(10), 1–5.

Chapter 2

TOWARDS SUSTAINABLE DEVELOPMENT: MEGAPROJECT SOCIAL RESPONSIBILITY AND STAKEHOLDER ENGAGEMENT

ABSTRACT: *This chapter looks at how megaprojects, for their complexity, costs and long-lasting impacts, must have a duty of care and social responsibility. For these reasons, the term Megaproject Social Responsibility (MSR) has been introduced by management scholars. Among other things, a good MSR approach entails moving from older conceptions of stakeholder identification, prioritization and management to relational approaches that take also into account the networks of stakeholders that gravitate around the project. In this chapter it is argued that attending these concerns and involving stakeholders early on, and throughout all phases of the megaproject, will contribute to its success.*

SUMMARY: 2.1. Introduction. – 2.2. The social responsibilities of megaprojects. – 2.3. Towards a relational stakeholder theory for megaproject management. – 2.4. Managing stakeholders in megaprojects. – 2.5. Summary. – *References.*

2.1. Introduction

The sustainable management of large-scale projects will be crucial for the planning and development of future infrastructure. Moving forward, embracing an ecosystem-based approach to sustainability is, and will be, the only acceptable construction paradigm (Flyvbjerg, 2014, 2017; Oliomogbe & Smith, 2012; Van Marrewijk et al., 2008). It must be acknowledged the importance of large infrastructure to achieve the United Nations Sustainable Development Goals, and the sustainable management of new infrastructure is further emphasized by the United Nations' Agenda 2030, specifically by SDG 9 on Innovation and Infrastructure (United Nations, 2020). However, their construction phase (as well as the planning one) may initially pose serious sustainability challenges that societies must necessarily take into account, especially when weighing the option of not building anything or maintaining the status quo (The New Climate Economy, 2016; United Nations, 2016).

Transportation-related megaprojects are particularly intertwined with sustainability issues, as global transportation accounts for 60% of total carbon emissions. To reverse this trend, there is an estimated global need for less environmentally impactful infrastructure, with railways alone requiring an investment of $7.9 trillion from 2017 to 2035 (Woetzel et al., 2017). While new investments in these projects may signal a tangible progress towards the achievement of SDGs, the construction phase raises various ethical concerns. These include the potential for social and environmental injustices, cost overruns, failure to meet project timelines, corruption, neglection of safety measures, conflicts with local communities, and disagreements (Li et al., 2013; Temper et al., 2015, 2018; Flyvbjerg, 2017; Bhatacharya et al., 2016; Cuganesan & Floris, 2020). To address these challenges, academics and decision-makers have focused on promoting the concept of Megaproject Social Responsibility (MSR) (Ma et al., 2017; Lin et al., 2017), defined by Zeng et al. (2015) as *"the policies and practices of stakeholders through the whole project lifecycle that reflect responsibilities for the well-being of the wide society"*. Building from this, Lin et al. (2017) argue that, taking a much-needed holistic perspective when it comes to assessing the social responsibility of megaprojects, the concepts of life-cycle dynamism, stakeholder heterogeneity, and social responsibility interactivity must be integrated. The need for an integrated perspective should not come as a surprise, if we consider that megaprojects have a substantial degree of complexity due to their size, long timeframes, high uncertainty, big number of stakeholders involved and intricate administrative structures (Lezak et al., 2019; Mok et al., 2015). One of the most challenging aspects of sustainable project management is the integration of stakeholder concerns into the design and implementation of these interventions (Winch, 2017; Eskerod & Ang, 2017; Williams et al., 2015; Eskerod & Huemann, 2013). According to traditional stakeholder theory, stakeholders encompass individuals and groups who can influence or be influenced by a company's operations (Freeman, 2010; Freeman & McVea, 2005). Stakeholders range from primary actors like project managers, contractors, investors, and policymakers (traditionally considered within the project management literature), to broader groups (more recently considered in academic literature), such as public institutions, citizens, local NGOs, and opponents (Karlsen, 2002; Mahmoudi et al., 2021; Aaltonen et al., 2008; Pizzi et al., 2021).

The identification of stakeholders is universally acknowledged by MSR scholars as a critical step for project success. This process should favor the adoption of a relational approach, analyzing the relationships between external stakeholders, internal stakeholders, and other relevant actors (Rowley, 2017). It is therefore essential to move beyond the traditional business-stakeholder relationships and explore concepts of sustainable development and environmental conservation (Steurer, 2006; Byrson, 2004). As the world becomes increasingly interconnected, stakeholder analysis gains strategic importance, particularly considering the interconnected nature of the SDGs (Allen et al., 2019; Byrson, 2004).

Managing the complexity of stakeholder identification, prioritization (if and when it is needed) and engagement, poses significant challenges for project managers (Davis et al., 2010), and addressing them requires going beyond simplistic stakeholder salience models and developing comprehensive strategies (Mitchell et al., 1997; Bondy and Charles, 2020). There is a recognized need for novel relational perspectives in stakeholder management, such as the Business2Nature (B2N) school of thought (Kujala and Korhonen, 2017). B2N, among different things, suggests considering the environment itself as a stakeholder. Other possible relational approaches include the use of social network analysis (SNA) to analyze the dynamic evolution of stakeholder ecosystems (Rowley, 2017) and the stakeholder social capital model (Cots, 2011).

2.2. The social responsibilities of megaprojects

It should be clear at this point that megaprojects have long-lasting, or even dramatic and permanent (Lin et. A., 2017) environmental, social, political and economic impacts (Wang et al, 2017; van Marrewijk et al. 2008; Flyvbjerg 2014, 2017). However, the focus on megaproject social responsibilities is still superficial, if compared to the attention given to CSR (Ma et al., 2017). As well as being extremely complex, megaprojects are also very dynamic, and these are some of the reasons behind the disparity in focus and attention between MSR and CSR. The way that dynamism is manifested during megaprojects' life-cycle involves not only an evolution of the various issues so far discussed but, importantly, a change in terms of primary participants and stakeholders over time, with different needs that emerge and networks that evolve as the project progresses (Ma et al., 2017). One of the goals of MSR is indeed understanding how to strike a reasonable balance among different stakeholder interests in megaprojects (Ma et al., 2019).

The holistic approach taken by MSR necessarily requires cooperation among several actors, rather than resting on a single company or few individuals (Ma et al., 2017). MSR strives to positively affect megaproject performance, but also to influence the strategies of other companies in the construction industry and the relations with the public sector (Ma et al., 2019, Tinoco et al., 2016; Hosseini et al., 2018, Mok et al., 2015). He et al. (2019) argue that MSR is indeed a reliable way to integrate all the aspects discussed above into project activities, and to contribute to the project's sustainable development, organizational, financial and non-financial success. They continue by affirming that adopting a socially responsible approach to megaprojects in the whole project can also spur innovation, which in turn helps in contributing to megaprojects' sustainable development (Chen et al., 2018, Zhou & Mi, 2017).

To provide more structure to MSR, its different dimensions and influence, Ma et al. (2019) elaborate a comprehensive model. Ranging from project level, to organizational and industrial, they first look at the different MSR dimensions (economic and quality, legal and regulatory, environmental and ethical, political and communal); then they move to the organizational level, accounting for the stakeholders involved (with a distinction between primary and secondary) and finally to the industrial level, looking at the sustainability improvements that MSR can bring (economic, environmental and social). They list an improved sharing of knowledge among primary stakeholders and a better industrial market and institutional environment for secondary stakeholders (Figure 1).

Figure 1. MSR framework

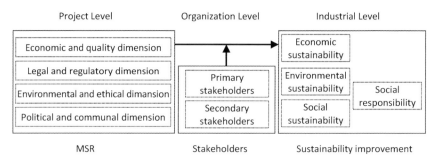

Source: Ma et al., 2019.

We believe that this model, while in line with the holistic perspective of MSR, could benefit from a less clear-cut approach to stakeholder identification and mapping. In the next section, we present how the academic literature on stakeholder theory has moved from salience approaches to more relational ones.

2.3. Towards a relational stakeholder theory for megaproject management

In recent times, numerous authors have emphasized the significance of shifting the focus of stakeholder theory from a transactional approach, centered around issue-solving, to a relational theoretical approach that prioritizes managing relationships (Vos & Achterkamp, 2015). This is due to placing too much attention to transactional approaches, leading practitioners to favor managerial tools that prioritize specific stakeholder categories and their interests, rather than embracing inclusive and democratic approaches (Mitchell et al., 1997; Kujala et al., 2019). Consequently, this has sometimes resulted in a great polarization of stakeholder interests, marginalizing certain categories while exaggerating others in the decision-making processes that benefit businesses (Kujala and Korhonen, 2017). More recently, even the advocates of stakeholders' salience have revised their stance, wishing for a more pluralistic conception and a value-creation process oriented towards the existence (and needs of) multiple stakeholders. In this process, stakeholders are regarded as active participants toward the co-creation of value (Mitchell et al., 2016; Wood et al., 2021; Mitchell & Lee, 2019).

Considering the increasing importance of sustainability science and the concept of socio-ecological services and ecosystems (Small et al., 2022), a clear identification of stakeholder networks has become a crucial step for organizations that strive to create value for their stakeholders and genuinely consider their perspectives in the decision-making process (Cottafava & Corazza, 2020). Embracing an ecosystem perspective means recognizing and including stakeholders who are not contractually linked to the focal company. This requires the identification of indirect stakeholders, a deep understanding of their interrelations, and acknowledging the presence of involuntary stakeholders (Byrson, 2004). Wood et al. (2021) clarify this point by stating that understanding and explaining stakeholder relationships (of all kinds) should be a natural consequence of the increasing scholarly efforts on business ethics.

Several scholars have significantly contributed to the shift in stakeholder identification and emphasized the importance of relationships. These include the works of Rowley (1997), Rowley and Moldoveanu (2003), Rowley (2017), Cots (2011), Steurer (2006), and the Business2Nature school of thought (Kujala & Korhonen, 2017; Kujala et al., 2012, Heikkinen et al., 2013; Kujala et al., 2016). Rowley (1997) was one of the pioneers in proposing a revision of the firm-centric model of stakeholder identification, toward a network-oriented approach. His model allows for the inclusion of indirect stakeholders and their visualization using Social Network Analysis (SNA) techniques (Mok et al., 2015). In Rowley's later work (2017), the concept of an ecosystem becomes even more prominent, incorporating interactions across different geographical scales and time periods into the evolving model. This addition provides valuable insights into the managerial implications of stakeholder mapping in long-term megaprojects that span decades. Managers of such projects need to consider current, future, and potential stakeholders at various scales, from local to national and even supranational levels. Hence, the "names-and-faces" approach (McVea & Freeman (2005) becomes relevant for its focus on individual relationships over generic classification of stakeholder groups. To be effective, this approach should be implemented at different scales and project sites, enhancing project managers' understanding of local communities and opponents over time. Therefore, it should help mitigate the risk of overestimating the resolution of specific disagreements, as managers gain a greater awareness of the stakeholders they interact with, particularly in highly adversarial relationships (Leung et al., 2005).

In the work of Cots (2011), a new normative model of stakeholder relationships is developed, grounded in the concept of social capital. The paper presents four perspectives: *structural,* focusing on the intensity of firm-stakeholder relationships; *relational,* centered around trust and norms of reciprocity; *cognitive,* involving the identification of a shared purpose toward a constructive dialogue; *evaluative,* linked to the contribution to the common good. While the study sheds light on different normative applications of stakeholder relationality and their benefits, it lacks a thorough discussion on conflict resolution, especially when relationships become irreconcilably polarized between opponents and proponents. This scenario is quite common in megaprojects, particularly when stakeholders are not engaged at an early stage (Olander, 2007). Conversely, Cots's paper offers intriguing insights into the significance of creating awareness among managers about the existence and composition of stakeholder networks. The paper emphasizes the development of meta-cognitive skills to effectively interact with these networks, moving beyond a limited dyadic view of the organization-stakeholder relationships.

Another valuable contribution comes from Steurer (2006), who proposes a comprehensive framework to highlight the diverse approaches employed in stakeholder analysis. His framework is based on a three-level perspective (corporate, stakeholder, and conceptual) and on the classification of Donaldson and Preston (1995) that distinguishes normative, instrumental, and descriptive theories, enabling a progression from a firm-centric descriptive analysis to normative and conceptual analyses. The descriptive aspect focuses on understanding "what does happen?", the instrumental aspect explores "what would happen if?", while the normative aspect addresses "what should happen?". These aspects collectively transform an analysis from a static snapshot of stakeholders to an ethical and moral assessment. Moreover, the framework incorporates three perspectives: firm-centric, stakeholder-centric, and conceptual. The firm-centric perspective examines how an organization impacts its stakeholders, the stakeholder-centric perspective explores how stakeholders influence the organization, and the conceptual perspective delves into the interrelationships and influences of specific concepts like sustainable development, biodiversity conservation, climate change, and the common good on the relationships between an organization and its stakeholders (Steurer, 2006). Shifting from a corporate-centric and descriptive analysis to a conceptual and normative approach is crucial for developing long-term sustainable strategies. This reasoning and stakeholder perspective, particularly in the conceptual and normative aspects, holds great significance in the planning and management of megaprojects, as it enables democratic dialogues, especially with secondary stakeholders such as environmental NGOs, who have traditionally acted as guardians and watchdogs for environmental preservation (Atkins et al., 2021).

The Finnish school of thought of Business2Nature takes a significant leap forward by focusing on the profound relationship within socio-ecological ecosystems, viewing Nature from a holistic and ecosystem perspective (Kujala & Korhonen, 2017). According to this approach, strategic management and stakeholder analysis should not only consider traditional stakeholders, but also include Nature, adopting a dynamic and multilevel approach and considering the interplay between the natural and built environment and stakeholders (Kujala et al., 2012; Heikkinen et al., 2013). Under this perspective, each territory possesses a distinct identity. Therefore, elements such as water resources, land use, environmental quality, and biodiversity preservation should be integral parts of stakeholder analysis. This is because societies and economies are deeply intertwined with place-based ecosystem services (Heikkinen et al., 2019). When it comes to developing megaprojects, particularly those with construction phases spanning several decades, planners and managers must develop an understanding of the ecosystem functioning within the territories and populations involved. This understanding goes beyond a socio-demographic analysis and recognizes Nature as a pivotal element in the relationships between local stakeholders and Nature itself, potentially acting as an influential participant. This perspective becomes even more crucial in the context of greenfield megaprojects, where the ecological environment undoubtedly experiences irreversible impacts that need to be adequately mitigated and compensated for.

2.4. Managing stakeholders in megaprojects

In the realm of project and megaproject management, the term "project stakeholders" is commonly used instead of "business stakeholders", as outlined by Aaltonen et al. (2008). A seminal work on stakeholder involvement in projects and megaprojects was presented by Karlsen (2002), emphasizing a pragmatic and instrumental approach to stakeholder management. This approach entailed classifying stakeholders to prioritize their involvement, excluding certain stakeholders, and proactively addressing uncertainties and potential problems. Expanding on this concept, Newcombe (2003) introduced a more comprehensive perspective on stakeholder inclusion, moving beyond a client-centric focus to embrace a pluralistic view. The paper introduced two models for mapping and classifying stakeholders: the power/predictability matrix and the power/interest matrix, derived from the work of Eden and Ackermann (1998). These models provide frameworks for analyzing stakeholder dynamics. Additionally, the paper presented two key principles for stakeholder management. The first principle emphasizes the significance of the interests and benefits of all stakeholders, particularly in the context of long-term construction projects. The second principle highlights the role of project managers as intermediaries, as a bridge between stakeholders and the project itself.

Over the subsequent decades, scholars delved into a thorough examination of the essential phases of stakeholder engagement, including identification, mapping, classification, and prioritization. They explored the associated challenges within the strategic management domain and sought to uncover the potential value that such engagement brings to companies (Aaltonen et al., 2008). However, it is worth noting that only recently researchers have begun to question the linear nature of the stakeholder engagement process. They have stressed the significance of incorporating dynamism into the equation, acknowledging that stakeholder dynamics can evolve and change over time. This recognition adds a new layer of complexity to stakeholder engagement practices. Park et al. (2017) provide a notable example in their work, focusing on long-term complex construction megaprojects. They underline that for project managers it is fundamental to continually reconsider the identification and prioritization of stakeholders throughout the project's entire duration. This is due to the inherent and inevitable changes that naturally unfold over the usually long time-span of the project. The authors call for a dynamic approach to stakeholder management, acknowledging the evolving nature of stakeholder relationships. In Yang's study (2014), the identification and prioritization phases of stakeholder engagement are examined utilizing Social Network Analysis (SNA) and the Stakeholder Circle methodology. This approach allows for a comprehensive understanding of the stakeholders involved, their relationships, and their relative importance within the project context. By employing these analytical tools, Yang explores the complexities of stakeholder dynamics and facilitates more informed decision-making regarding stakeholder engagement strategies. For the scholar, the value of Social Network

Analysis (SNA) lies in cases where it is necessary to establish a priori knowledge of the stakeholder network and identify reciprocal relationships among stakeholders. Moreover, by visualizing these complex relationships, and going beyond dyadic bonds (Mok et. al, 2015), it becomes possible to elucidate how value is created within stakeholder interactions, as emphasized by Myllykangas et al. (2010).

As highlighted by Davis et al. (2010), the specific context in which a project operates plays a significant role in shaping the interactions among different stakeholders. Traditional stakeholder models often fail to account for the diverse levels at which stakeholders operate, such as institutional, media, opinion, cultural, and political realms. Moreover, these models may overlook the internal dimension of stakeholders, which encompasses individuals directly involved in project execution. It is fundamental to identify internal stakeholders who hold crucial and pivotal roles in achieving project objectives. On the other hand, external stakeholders, as explained by Beringer et al. (2013), do not have a direct and official contractual relationship with the project but can still exert influence on its outcomes. These external stakeholders may impact the project through their actions, opinions, or interests, making their engagement and management essential for project success. By recognizing the distinction between internal and external stakeholders and understanding their unique roles and influences, project managers can develop more effective strategies to engage and collaborate with stakeholders across both dimensions. Within the existing literature, there is recognition of the importance of engaging secondary stakeholders early on in a project (Olander, 2007; Aaltonen 2011), creating spaces for empowerment and for an open dialogue (Rowlinson & Cheung, 2008). However, in practice, stakeholders are often only considered after crucial decisions have already been made, which can easily lead to controversies and, in some cases, even violent reactions and protests, as highlighted by Nederhand & Klijn (2019) and Schormair & Gilbert (2021). To better understand the complex dynamics of stakeholder relationships in highly contested projects, managers should invest time and resources to grasp and assess the stakeholder ecosystems and the interactions within their social network (Rowlinson & Cheung, 2008). By better grasping these dynamics, project managers can proactively address potential conflicts, identify influential stakeholders, and foster effective communication and collaboration among stakeholders. Moreover, this proactive approach to stakeholder engagement can contribute to mitigating controversies early on and enhancing the project outcomes overall.

2.5. Summary

This chapter has attempted to address some of the complex and challenging issues of managing stakeholders in light of the sustainable development of megaprojects, which has received extensive attention in the literature on Megaproject Social Responsibility (MSR). Megaprojects, particularly those in the realm of infrastructure, involve a vast array of stakeholders who often lack an adequate representation and voice in decision-making processes. Additionally, in line with the Sustainable Development Goals (SDGs), now more than ever it is extremely important to take into account nature and the natural environment, as advocated by the Business2Nature literature.

The chapter has begun by analyzing the concept of MSR and its growing relevance. Then, it has traced the trajectory from more traditional versions of stakeholder theory, such as those proposed by Freeman (1984) and Mitchell et al. (1997), to relational approaches (e.g., Rowley, 2017), better suited to represent stakeholder issues in megaprojects. Finally, the chapter has highlighted some of the issues in managing stakeholder in (often contested) megaprojects, to avoid fights and protests and ultimately contributing to sustainable development objectives.

References

Aaltonen, K. (2011). Project stakeholder analysis as an environmental interpretation process. *International journal of project management*, 29(2), 165–183.

Aaltonen, K., Jaakko, K. & Tuomas, O. (2008). Stakeholder salience in global projects. *International journal of project management*, 26(5), 509–516.

Beringer, C., Jonas, D. & Kock, A. (2013). Behavior of internal stakeholders in project portfolio management and its impact on success. *International journal of project management*, 31(6), 830–846.

Bhattacharya, A., Meltzer, J.P., Oppenheim, J., Qureshi, Z. & Stern, N. (2022, March 9). Delivering on sustainable infrastructure for better development and better climate. *Brookings*. https://www.brookings.edu/research/delivering-on-sustainable-infrastructure-for-better-development-and-better-climate/.

Bryson, J.M. (2004). What to do when stakeholders matter: stakeholder identification and analysis techniques. *Public management review*, 6(1), 21–53.

Chen, H., Su, Q., Zeng, S., Sun, D. & Shi, J.J. (2018). Avoiding the innovation island in infrastructure mega-project. *Frontiers of Engineering Management*, 5(1), 109–124.

Cots, E.G. (2011). Stakeholder social capital: a new approach to stakeholder theory. *Business Ethics: A European Review*, 20(4), 328–341.

Cottafava, D. & Corazza, L. (2020). Co-design of a stakeholders' ecosystem: An assessment methodology by linking social network analysis, stakeholder theory and participatory mapping. *Kybernetes*, 50(3), 836–858.

Cuganesan, S. & Floris, M. (2020). Investigating perspective taking when infrastructure megaproject teams engage local communities: Navigating tensions and balancing perspectives. *International Journal of Project Management*, 38(3), 153–164.

Davis, J., MacDonald, A. & White, L. (2010). Problem-structuring methods and project management: an example of stakeholder involvement using Hierarchical Process Modelling methodology. *Journal of the Operational Research Society*, 61(6), 893–904.

Donaldson, T. & Preston, L.E. (1995). The stakeholder theory of the corporation: Concepts, evidence, and implications. *Academy of management Review*, 20(1), 65–91.

Eden, C. & Ackermann, F. (1998). *Making strategy: The journey of strategic management*. Sage.

Eskerod, P. & Ang, K. (2017). Stakeholder value constructs in megaprojects: A long-term assessment case study. *Project Management Journal*, 48(6), 60–75.

Eskerod, P. & Huemann, M. (2013). Sustainable development and project stakeholder management: What standards say. *International Journal of Managing Projects in Business*, 6(1), 36–50.

Flyvbjerg, B. (2014). What you should know about megaprojects and why: An overview. *Project management journal*, 45(2), 6–19.

Flyvbjerg, B. (Ed.). (2017). *The Oxford handbook of megaproject management*. Oxford University Press.

Freeman, R.E. (2010). *Strategic management: A stakeholder approach*. Cambridge University Press.

He, Q., Chen, X., Wang, G., Zhu, J., Yang, D., Liu, X. & Li, Y. (2019). Managing social responsibility for sustainability in megaprojects: An innovation transitions perspective on success. *Journal of Cleaner Production*, 241, 118395.

Heikkinen, A., Kujala, J. & Lehtimäki, H. (2013). Managing stakeholder dialogue: The case of Botnia in Uruguay. *South Asian Journal of Business and Management Cases*, 2(1), 25–37.

Heikkinen, A., Nieminen, J., Kujala, J., Mäkelä, H., Jokinen, A. & Lehtonen, O. (2019). Stakeholder engagement in the generation of urban ecosystem services. *Leading change in a complex world: Transdisciplinary perspectives*. Tampere University Press.

Hosseini, M.R., Banihashemi, S., Martek, I., Golizadeh, H. & Ghodoosi, F. (2018). Sustainable delivery of megaprojects in Iran: Integrated model of contextual factors. *Journal of Management in Engineering*, 34(2), 05017011.

Karlsen, J.T. (2002). Project stakeholder management. *Engineering management journal*, 14(4), 19–24.

Kujala, J., Heikkinen, A. & Lehtimäki, H. (2012). Understanding the nature of stakeholder relationships: An empirical examination of a conflict situation. *Journal of business ethics*, 109, 53–65.

Kujala, J., Lehtimäki, H. & Myllykangas, P. (2016). Toward a relational stakeholder theory: Attributes of value-creating stakeholder relationships. In *Academy of Management Proceedings*. Vol. 2016, No. 1, 13609. Academy of Management.

Kujala, J. & Korhonen, A. (2017). Value-creating stakeholder relationships in the context of CSR. In *Stakeholder engagement: Clinical research cases*. Vol 46. Springer, 63–85.

Kujala, J., Lehtimäki, H. & Freeman, E.R. (2019). A stakeholder approach to value creation and leadership. In *Leading change in a complex world: Transdisciplinary perspectives*. Tampere University Press, 123-144

Leung, M.Y., Liu, A.M. & Ng, S.T. (2005). Is there a relationship between construction conflicts and participants' satisfaction? *Engineering, Construction and Architectural Management*, 12(2), 149–167.

Lezak, S., Ahearn, A., McConnell, F. & Sternberg, T. (2019). Frameworks for conflict mediation in international infrastructure development: A comparative overview and critical appraisal. *Journal of Cleaner Production*, 239, 118099.

Li, K., Zhu, C., Wu, L. & Huang, L. (2013). Problems caused by the Three Gorges Dam construction in the Yangtze River basin: a review. *Environmental Reviews*, 21(3), 127–135.

Lin, H., Zeng, S., Ma, H., Zeng, R. & Tam, V.W. (2017). An indicator system for evaluating megaproject social responsibility. *International Journal of Project Management*, 35(7), 1415–1426.

Ma, H., Zeng, S., Lin, H., Chen, H. & Shi, J.J. (2017). The societal governance of megaproject social responsibility. *International Journal of Project Management*, 35(7), 1365–1377.

Ma, H., Liu, Z., Zeng, S., Lin, H. & Tam, V.W. (2020). Does megaproject social responsibility improve the sustainability of the construction industry? *Engineering, Construction and Architectural Management*, 27(4), 975–996.

Mahmoudi, A., Deng, X., Javed, S.A. & Zhang, N. (2021). Sustainable supplier selection in megaprojects: grey ordinal priority approach. *Business Strategy and The Environment*, 30(1), 318–339.

McVea, J.F. & Freeman, R.E. (2005). A names-and-faces approach to stakeholder management: How focusing on stakeholders as individuals can bring ethics and entrepreneurial strategy together. *Journal of management inquiry*, 14(1), 57–69.

Mitchell, R.K., Agle, B.R. & Wood, D.J. (1997). Toward a theory of stakeholder identification and salience: Defining the principle of who and what really counts. *Academy of management review*, 22(4), 853–886.

Mitchell, R.K. & Lee, J.H. (2019). Stakeholder identification and its importance in the value creating system of stakeholder work. In *The Cambridge handbook of stakeholder theory*. Vol. 1. Cambridge University Press, 53–73.

Mitchell, R.K., Weaver, G.R., Agle, B.R., Bailey, A.D. & Carlson, J. (2016). Stakeholder agency and social welfare: Pluralism and decision making in the multi-objective corporation. *Academy of Management review*, 41(2), 252–275.

Mok, K.Y., Shen, G.Q. & Yang, J. (2015). Stakeholder management studies in mega construction projects: A review and future directions. *International journal of project management*, 33(2), 446–457.

Myllykangas, P., Kujala, J. & Lehtimäki, H. (2010). Analyzing the essence of stakeholder relationships: What do we need in addition to power, legitimacy, and urgency? *Journal of Business Ethics*, 96, 65–72.

Nederhand, J. & Klijn, E.H. (2019). Stakeholder involvement in public–private partnerships: Its influence on the innovative character of projects and on project performance. *Administration & Society*, 51(8), 1200–1226.

Newcombe, R. (2003). From client to project stakeholders: a stakeholder mapping approach. *Construction management and economics*, 21(8), 841–848.

Olander, S. (2007). Stakeholder impact analysis in construction project management. *Construction management and economics*, 25(3), 277–287.

Oliomogbe, G. & Smith, J.N. (2012). Value in megaprojects. *Organization, technology & management in construction: an international journal*, 4(3), 617–24.

Park, H., Kim, K., Kim, Y.W. & Kim, H. (2017). Stakeholder management in long-term complex megaconstruction projects: The Saemangeum project. *Journal of Management in Engineering*, 33(4), 05017002.

Pizzi, S., Moggi, S., Caputo, F. & Rosato, P. (2021). Social media as stakeholder engagement tool: CSR communication failure in the oil and gas sector. *Corporate Social Responsibility and Environmental Management*, 28(2), 849–859.

Rowley, T.J. (1997). Moving beyond dyadic ties: A network theory of stakeholder influences. *Academy of management Review*, 22(4), 887–910.

Rowley, T.J. (2017). The power of and in stakeholder networks. In *Stakeholder Management*. Vol. 1. Emerald Publishing Limited, 101–122.

Rowley, T.I. & Moldoveanu, M. (2003). When will stakeholder groups act? An interest-and identity-based model of stakeholder group mobilization. *Academy of management review*, 28(2), 204–219.

Rowlinson, S. & Cheung, Y.K.F. (2008). Stakeholder management through empowerment: modelling project success. *Construction Management and Economics*, 26(6), 611–623.

Schormair, M.J. & Gilbert, D.U. (2021). Creating value by sharing values: Managing stakeholder value conflict in the face of pluralism through discursive justification. *Business Ethics Quarterly*, 31(1), 1–36.

Small, A., Owen, A. & Paavola, J. (2022). Organizational use of ecosystem service approaches: A critique from a systems theory perspective. *Business Strategy and the Environment*, 31(1), 284–296.

Steurer, R. (2006). Mapping stakeholder theory anew: from the 'stakeholder theory of the firm' to three perspectives on business-society relations. *Business strategy and the environment*, 15(1), 55–69.

Temper, L., Del Bene, D. & Martinez-Alier, J. (2015). Mapping the frontiers and front lines of global environmental justice: the EJAtlas. *Journal of Political Ecology*, 22(1), 255–278.

Temper, L., Demaria, F., Scheidel, A., Del Bene, D. & Martinez-Alier, J. (2018). The Global Environmental Justice Atlas (EJAtlas): ecological distribution conflicts as forces for sustainability. *Sustainability Science*, 13(3), 573–584.

The New Climate Economy (2016). The sustainable infrastructure imperative: financing for better growth and development. https://newclimateeconomy.re port/2016/.

Tinoco, R.A., Sato, C.E.Y. & Hasan, R. (2016). Responsible project management: beyond the triple constraints. *The Journal of Modern Project Management*, 4(1), 179–179.

Van Marrewijk, A., Clegg, S.R., Pitsis, T.S. & Veenswijk, M. (2008). Managing public-private megaprojects: Paradoxes, complexity, and project design. *International journal of project management*, 26(6), 591–600.

Vos, J. & Achterkamp, M.C. (2015). Bridging the transactional and relational view on management-stakeholder cooperation. *International Journal of Organizational Analysis*, 23(4), 652–663.

Wang, G., He, Q., Meng, X., Locatelli, G., Yu, T. & Yan, X. (2017). Exploring the impact of megaproject environmental responsibility on organizational citizenship behaviors for the environment: A social identity

perspective. *International Journal of Project Management*, *35*(7), 1402–1414.
Williams, N.L., Ferdinand, N. & Pasian, B. (2015). Online stakeholder interactions in the early stage of a megaproject. *Project Management Journal*, *46*(6), 92–110.
Winch, G. (2017). *Megaproject Stakeholder Management*. Oxford University Press eBooks.
Woetzel, J., Garemo, N., Mischke, J., Kamra, P., Palter, R. (2017). *Bridging infrastructure gaps: Has the world made progress?* McKinsey & Company. https://www.mckinsey.com/capabilities/operations/ourinsights/bridging-infrastructure-gaps-has-the-world-made-progress.
Wood, D.J., Mitchell, R.K., Agle, B.R. & Bryan, L.M. (2021). Stakeholder identification and salience after 20 years: Progress, problems, and prospects. *Business & Society*, *60*(1), 196–245.
United Nations (2016). Mobilizing Sustainable Transport for Development. https://sustainabledevelopment.un.org/content/documents/2375Mobilizing%20Sustainable%20Transport.pdf.
United Nations (2020). *The Sustainable Development Agenda*. https://www.un.org/sustainabledevelopment/development-agenda/.
Zeng, S.X., Ma, H.Y., Lin, H., Zeng, R.C. & Tam, V.W. (2015). Social responsibility of major infrastructure projects in China. *International journal of project management*, *33*(3), 537–548.
Zhou, Z. & Mi, C. (2017). Social responsibility research within the context of megaproject management: Trends, gaps and opportunities. *International Journal of Project Management*, *35*(7), 1378–1390.

Chapter 3

CRITICAL INFRASTRUCTURE AND SUSTAINABLE DEVELOPMENT: A PARADOXICAL LINK

ABSTRACT: *What relationship exists between critical infrastructure and sustainable development? What paradoxes does critical infrastructure imply and why are they the solution but also a hindering factor to the social, environmental and economic problems to which they should contribute? This chapter will address the links between megaprojects, critical infrastructure and their contribution to sustainable development.*

SUMMARY: 3.1. Introduction. – 3.2. Defining critical infrastructure. – 3.3. Mapping the research field on critical infrastructure sector and climate change. – 3.4. Mapping the field on critical infrastructure and SDGs. – 3.5. A benchmark analysis of critical infrastructural megaprojects in the transportation sector. – 3.5.1. Methodology. – 3.5.2. Impacts mentioned in the reports and connection to SDGs. – 3.6. Summary. – 3.7. Annex I: list of impacts. – *References*.

3.1. Introduction

Low-GHG transitions that are also resistant to the effects of climate change will be a future necessity for new global infrastructure. Decisions made now will lock in vulnerability if these effects are not already taken into account during the design phase, because infrastructure assets have a long lifespan. The size of investment decisions is substantial. According to the OECD, infrastructure investment globally between 2016 and 2030 will need to increase by USD 6.3 trillion annually to keep up with development (OECD, 2017).

These figures do not account neither for the true financial impact brought on by the investments required for infrastructure mitigation and adaptation, nor for the possible contributions of such infrastructure for sustainable development. In light of this, the purpose of this chapter is to contribute to the current literature by exploring the relationship between Critical Infrastructure (CI) and sustainable development. In particular, this paper is concentrated on a subcategory of infrastructure, namely critical infrastructure, which play a crucial role in socioeconomic systems. It should be noted that CI are not always megaprojects, but CI and megaprojects share specific features.

3.2. Defining critical infrastructure

Critical infrastructure is a pivotal element in the functioning of a specific country's economy, as they guarantee a certain level of social prosperity. They are defined as critical because a malfunction or damage to these infrastructure *systems* could disrupt an essential service to a nation. CI are defined as tangible and intangible systems and assets that provide a country with an essential service, and whose disruption could generate security, economic stability, public health, safety, or various concatenated problems.

Although this concept originated in the 1990s in the USA, critical infrastructure is of critical importance on every continent. There is also a specific legislative proposal in Europe designed to invite individual member states to identify those infrastructure systems that may represent a material level of criticality in maintaining vital societal functions, as their "disruption or destruction would have a significant impact in a Member State as a result of the failure to maintain those functions" (European Commission, 2008).

The notion of criticality is thus related to the possibility that temporary or permanent damage may stop the operation of the infrastructure. In this sense then, criticality is seen as vulnerability (Egan, 2007; P.R. Schulman & Roe, 2007; P. Schulman, Roe, Van Eeten & De Bruijne, 2015). Vulnerability is thus understood to be the relationship between two elements related to the notion of risk: the predictability of a given risk occurring, and the severity of the associated consequences, which could impact the functioning of CI.

Regarding the predictability perspective, thus, there are different types of risks, from those that are technical and human-dependent, such as terrorist attacks (Boin & Smith, 2006), to risks that are more related to socio-environmental systems, and natural and meteorological, as in the case of earthquakes and tidal waves (Kumar, Poonia, Gupta & Goyal, 2021). Both categories represent different degrees of predictability. Regarding the associated consequences, they could be analyzed according to a short-term or long-term perspective.

Direct impact issues, i.e., when the infrastructure is damaged, may result in a temporary, or prolonged suspension of the service offered. Permanent and irreversible damage results in complete disruption that may persist over time. In addition, a further difference exists between direct impacts and indirect impacts, i.e., the series of malfunctions and disruptions that cascade to other related CI (Boin & McConnell, 2007; Ghorbani & Bagheri, 2008; Iturriza, Labaka, Sarriegi & Hernantes, 2018; Ouyang, 2014).

Further peculiar aspects of CI are also represented by the mutual interconnection between different infrastructure systems and the increasingly real possibility that the same CI can connect and impact the functioning of two or more states (AIIC, 2017). In the former case, the disruption of service of one CI, a sort of node (Cao & Lam, 2019), could directly impact the operation of other CIs connected to it through cascading (Boin & McConnell, 2007; De Bruijne, Van Eeten, Roe & Schulman, 2006). An example of this is the disruption of electrical services, which could slow down the operation of hospitals in a specific area. In the second case, reference is made to interconnections between different states, where therefore the CI represents a unifying element (Fritzon, Ljungkvist, Boin & Rhinard, 2007). For instance, in the case of a highway, tunnel, bridge, or rail line, interconnections between different states would also be disrupted, so the resulting impacts would go beyond the geographic boundaries of a specific nation.

A further aspect of interest, and which unites CI with megaprojects, is that often the governance and the financing of these are hybrid and fragmented (Cedergren, Lidell & Lidell, 2019; Knodt et al., 2021). There may be different types of CI governance, from public to entirely private, or to forms of public-private collaboration. Or again, some CI can be managed by different countries and their respective governments. Consequently, the governance of a CI is an essential feature for the social and political implications that derive from it, to increase the resilience of the systems themselves (Rehak, Senovsky, Hromada & Lovecek, 2019). Sometimes the decision-making process goes beyond a single state or a single institution but can connect business networks, or intergovernmental agreements (Wang, Xu, He, Chan & Owusu, 2022).

Financial and insurance aspects also become critical elements of CI. In particular, a CI has likely taken a long time to build and enter into operation, and the funding for its operation may likely concern different subjects, including supranational institutions, such as the European Union or the World Bank (Almeida, Trindade, Komljenovic & Finger, 2022; de Gooyert, 2020; van den Adel, de Vries & van Donk, 2022). A summary of the main features of CI is depicted in Figure 1. After defining CI, in the next section, we will introduce a research perspective on the interplay between CI and climate change and CI and the Sustainable Development Goals (SDGs).

Figure 1. Salient elements of Critical Infrastructure

MAIN FEATURES OF CRITICAL INFRASTRUCTURES
Provide a country with an essential service.
A malfunction or damage to these infrastructures could disrupt an essential service to a nation.
Maintaining vital societal functions.
Criticality is seen in vulnerability: the predictability of a given risk occurring, and the severity of the associated consequences, which could impact the functioning of the CI.
Mutual interconnection between different infrastructures and the increasingly real possibility that the same CI can connect and impact the functioning of two or more states

Source: authors' own elaboration.

3.3. Mapping the research field on critical infrastructure sector and climate change

The research field of CI and sustainable development is still embryonic, but in rapid growth. In this volume, we adopt an interdisciplinary perspective matching sustainability science, sustainability accounting, sociology, physics that are all representing the different backgrounds of the authors of this book. Despite the different approaches and mindsets, it appears clear today how climate change could threaten the world and the populations of the (too near) future. However, the relevance of climate change impacts to global economies is certain and global infrastructure will not be an exception. CI are essential for achieving the SDGs, but an interruption due to climate change impacts could cause catastrophic consequences. As such, the impacts due to climate change represent one of the most plausible risks for CI development, investments and realizations. For instance, in August 2023, the functioning of some CI such as bridges, roads, and ports, have been seriously disrupted as a consequence of extreme weather events, like continuous droughts, wildfires, and hailstorms (see for references the problems experienced in the cargo transportation in China on the Yangtze, in USA on the Mississippi River, or the Panama Canal all affected by droughts). The rising in the sea levels or the coastal erosion are both a highly likely risk for all those CI that find their geographic location in coastal areas (like in the case of nuclear power plants, but also ports and oil/gas pipelines) (Hallegatte, Green, Nicholls & Corfee-Morlot, 2013). But also heatwaves, extreme weather events, floods, and storms could represent a source of risk for interrupting activities of CI (Intergovernmental Panel on Climate Change, 2022; Kumar et al., 2021; Mikellidou, Shakou, Boustras & Dimopoulos, 2018).

In this sense, the adoption of adaptation and mitigation strategies will become crucial for the strategic management of CI (Forzieri et al., 2018; Kumar et al., 2021).

Specifically, the vulnerability of a CI due to climate change may imply a different degree of temporality before a manager could directly see the direct consequences of adverse climatic impacts. In other words, there could be predictable and unpredictable events, but also events that occur with a high degree of chronicity over long periods, and events that occur with a degree of instantaneity that is often unpredictable and not chronic in the short term. The chronicity of the events directly impacts the climatic stress to which these infrastructure systems are subjected causing different degrees of urgency, from interruption of the operations to accelerating the degradation of the infrastructure itself and the materials (Liu, Fang & Zio, 2021; Zio, 2016a, 2016b). Next to instantaneous events, where therefore the rapidity of the occurrence of such an event is high, there are also slower and more protracted effects over time, which can then result in the permanent disruption of operation if not properly monitored (Achillopoulou, Mitoulis, Argyroudis & Wang, 2020; Argyroudis et al., 2020; Jönsson, 2010; Splichalova, Patrman, Kotalova & Hromada, 2020).

As a result, the resilience to climate change impacts is a crucial problem for managing CI, and during the design phase, architects and engineers should forecast such impacts while designing such projects. With this in mind, it appears clear that one of the tasks during the design phase in CI is increasing the robustness of a specific infrastructure to ensure its reliability and resilience (Rehak, Senovsky & Slivkova, 2018). Interruptions are still plausible, but working to increase resilience means increasing the ability of a CI to recover quickly and to return to a complete functioning, at the same level. This is done by absorbing the generating causes, ensuring that the risk of interruption decreases (prevention) over time and that the recovery time between one event and the next one progressively reduces (absorb, adapt, recover) in a predetermined way (Kamran, 2022). Therefore, CI resilience goes beyond CI protection implying a proper level of equipment in terms of robustness, redundancy, resourcefulness, and rapidity (Knodt, Fraune & Engel, 2021).

Specifically, therefore, decisions regarding the impacts deriving from climate change on CI may entail complex processes and are not easy to be implemented, requiring scenario analysis and multi-stakeholder consensus panels (Forzieri et al., 2016). Therefore, it implies that at a global level, the topic of climate-resilient infrastructure is a theme of timely importance and the scientific production on this topic is still growing (Coaffee & Clarke, 2017; OECD, 2018; Vallejo & Mullan, 2017). In Table 1, the relevant features of critical infrastructure are briefly synthesized adopting the implications due to climate change. Finally, multi-stakeholder engagement processes will also be essential in driving climate-resilient infrastructure pathways, as CI are mostly impacting citizens and communities that could participate locally in designing adaptation plans.

Table 1. Main features of CI and climate change implications

Purpose	Tangible and intangible systems and assets that provide a country with an essential service.
Operations	Disruption or destruction of a CI could generate security, economic stability, public health, safety, or various concatenated problems to economies and societies at local, regional, national, and also supra-national levels.
Sectors	Transportation systems, power and energy networks, water networks, and security infrastructure, hospitals, among others.
Vulnerability	The predictability of a given risk occurring, and the severity of the associated consequences. Consequences span from short-term to long-term. Temporary consequences vs permanent and irreversible damages. The temporality of unpredictable events versus slow but constant impacts.
Interconnection	CI as a node in complex networks. Cascading effect on other CIs and systems-of-systems. CI as interconnections between different countries.
Risk management	Technical and human-dependent risks (social nature of risks), as well as natural and meteorological risks. Adoption of preservation policies. Guarantee reliability and robustness.
Resilience	Going beyond reliability. Prevention, absorption, adaptation, recovery. Robustness, redundancy, resourcefulness, rapidity.
Governance	Funding and related decision-making (public, private, PPP, hybrids) and fragmented models. Inter-organizational decision-making with international implications.

Source: author's own elaboration on the literature review.

3.4. Mapping the field on critical infrastructure and SDGs

As the foundation of contemporary society and economies, CI are essential to accomplishing the SDGs set forth by the United Nations. Energy, transportation, water, and communication networks are among these fundamental systems that form the basis for sustainable development in a variety of industries. The following is a summary of their importance in furthering the SDGs:

- **Infrastructure for energy** (SDG 7: Access to Affordable and Clean Energy): To achieve sustainable development, it is essential to have access to dependable and clean energy. Critical energy infrastructure, such as renewable energy installations and effective networks, are crucial to encourage the adoption of clean energy, lowering greenhouse gas emissions, and guaranteeing that everyone has access to inexpensive energy.
- **Infrastructure in the field of transportation** (SDG 9: Industry, Innovation, and Infrastructure): Effective transportation systems are essential for fostering economic development, advancing industry, and tying communities together. Public transit and green mobility options are examples of sustainable transportation systems that lower emissions, expand accessibility, and enhance urban design.
- **Infrastructure for clean water and sanitation** (SDG 6): For the wellbeing of people and the preservation of the environment, access to clean water and sanitation is essential. To provide clean water, manage water resources, and reduce water-related diseases, critical water facilities, such as water treatment plants and distribution networks, are essential.
- **Infrastructure for communication** (SDG 9: Industry, Infrastructure, and Innovation): Information interchange, technological adoption, and innovation are all made possible by robust communication networks. By bridging the digital divide and encouraging inclusive growth, these infrastructure systems assist economic development, healthcare, education, and economic growth.
- **Disaster management and resilience** (SDG 11: Sustainable Cities and Communities): Critical infrastructure needs to be built to endure disruptions from natural disasters and other events. By creating resilient infrastructure, communities may quickly recover from catastrophes, lowering their susceptibility and promoting sustainable urban growth.
- **Employment matters related to megaprojects and critical infrastructure** (SDG 8: Decent Work and Economic Growth): Critical infrastructure investments boost economic activity and produce job opportunities. Sustainable infrastructure development creates jobs and promotes economic expansion, which reduces poverty and improves the quality of life.
- **Environmental Conservation** (interconnections between different SDGs): Strategic planning and management of vital infrastructure can reduce the negative effects on the environment. Several SDGs pertaining to en-

vironmental preservation, climate action, and biodiversity conservation are aided by the use of green technologies and sustainable practices in infrastructure construction.

3.5. A benchmark analysis of critical infrastructural megaprojects in the transportation sector

A mapping of large-scale works with characteristics similar to the Turin-Lyon case could be helpful for finding connections between impacts on SDGs. In particular, we used the studies produced within the European COST Megaproject (Brookes & Elmahroug, 2015), which presents a series of benchmarking precisely on large works, and from which common traits can be deduced. Specifically, eleven megaprojects have been analyzed, geographically distributed as per the attached cartography (Figure 2).

Figure 2. Cartography of the megaprojects analyzed, representing critical infrastructure

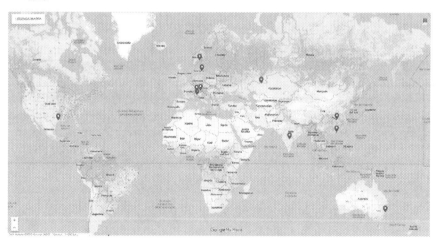

Source: authors' own elaboration on data collected for the benchmark.

According to the definition of CI, the projects were selected taking into account certain basic common features, such as:

– Binational or Tri-national;
– Critical infrastructure in the field of railways and related transportation;
– Highly environmental impacting projects (e.g. railway tunnels, etc.).

Obviously, not all the selected works perfectly match the case of the Turin-Lyon megaproject (see chapters 6 and 7), but in this study, a selection of projects with similarities or combinations of two or more simultaneous characteristics have been included. The type of infrastructure analyzed favors rail transport infrastructure, in which high-speed infrastructure, as well as tunnels and railway tunnels, are considered. Infrastructure such as motorways, roads, bridges, subways, and highway works were also considered, only when the extent of the works, works carried out in bi-national contexts, were of interest (see Table 2).

3.5.1. Methodology

The websites of the benchmarked megaprojects were analyzed with the aim of understanding which indicators are most promoted by the companies executing the works on their sites, and which are easily accessible. It should be noted that the intention of this study has been to map both positive and negative impacts as listed by the company responsible for the execution of the works. With this in mind, the paradoxical nature of the SDGs is evident as alongside negative impacts, we have noticed the presence of lists of positive impacts that go beyond eventual monetary compensations.

In addition, a further level of analysis has been established by collecting the sustainability reports of the companies included in the benchmark, that are signatories of the United Nations Global Compact (UNGC) publishing an updated Communication of Progress (CoP) or a Communication on Engagement (CoE). The reports included in this analysis are:

1. Acciona (Integrated Report 2018, Sustainability report 2019).
2. Arup (CoP 2019).
3. Autodesk (Sustainability report 2018 and Sustainability report 2019).
4. BBT SE (CoE 2016–2018).
5. China Railway (Social Responsibility report 2018).
6. Fincantieri (Sustainability report 2019).
7. Salini Impregilo (now WeBuild) (Sustainability report 2016).

The different areas of impact have been clustered into homogeneous categories that include, firstly, economic impacts, environmental impacts, and finally social and health and safety impacts. The list of impacts retrieved in the documents analyzed includes both positive and negative elements (Winch, 2017).

Table 2. Megaprojects used as a benchmark for the analysis of SDGs

Megaproject	Starting date	Estimated ending date	Country(ies)	Typologies
Genoa Bridge	2019	2020	Italy	Highway, bridge
Texas High Speed Rail	2020	2026	USA	Rail transport system
Brennero Tunnel	2007	2028	Austria and Italy	Railroad tunnel
Wuhan-Shiyan High-Speed Railway Line	2015	2019	China	Rail transport system
Galleria di Base del Monte Ceneri New Rail Link through the Alps (NRLA)	2006	2020	Switzerland	Railroad tunnel
Cityringen	2013	2019	Denmark	Subway
Sydney Metro Northwest	2008	2019	Australia	Subway
Hyderabad Metro Rail Network	2017	N/A	India	Subway
Hong Kong-Zhuhai-Macau Bridge	2009	2018	China, Hong Kong, Macau	Bridges, tunnels
South West Roads Project: Western Europe-Western China International Transit Corridor	2009	2015 (2021 for definitive project)	Kazakhstan	Restructuring and upgrading of rural and interurban roads
Follo Line	2015	2021	Norway	High-speed railway

Source: authors' own elaboration on the sample used as a benchmark.

3.5.2. Impacts mentioned in the reports and connection to SDGs

Through a content analysis of the dedicated websites and reports, a list of 82 different impacts has been discovered. Broad categories of impacts recall social, environmental, and economic impacts, plus an additional group composed of impacts on the health and safety conditions of populations and workers (see Annex I).

Critical infrastructure and sustainable development   **47**

According to the SDG mapper tool developed by the European Commission, the impacts included in the analysis have been processed to discover the main implications in terms of the SDGs (https://knowsdgs.jrc.ec.europa.eu/). From this analysis, 12 out of 17 SDGs have been found. SDG9 (Industry, Innovation, and Infrastructure) has been excluded from the analysis as it is the main theme of the entire work. Four SDGs have been the most cited: SDG8 (Decent Work and Economic Growth), SDG12 (Responsible Consumption and Production), SDG3 (Good Health and Well-Being), and SDG7 (Affordable and Clean Energy). Other SDGs mentioned are: SDG1 (No Poverty), SDG5 (Gender Equality), SDG6 (Clean Water and Sanitation), SDG10 (Reduced Inequalities), SDG11 (Reduced Inequalities), SDG13 (Climate Action), SDG15 (Life on Land), and SDG16 (Peace, Justice and Strong Institutions).

The only SDGs apparently excluded from the analysis have been SDG2 (Zero Hunger), SDG4 (Quality Education), and SDG 14 (Life Below Water). Please refer to Figure 3 for the entire overview of the SDGs most mentioned in our analysis.

Figure 3. List of the SDGs most mentioned according to the SDG Mapper tool of the European Commission

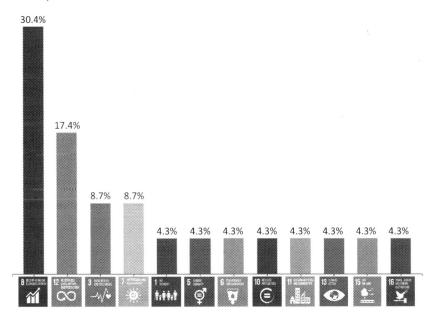

Source: authors' own elaboration on data retrieved from the sample processed by the SDG Mapper tool.

Specifically, according to a more in-depth view of the SDGs, some indicators are also aligned with specific targets (see Figure 4). From the analysis, it should be noted that this mapping exercise could be one of the starting points for a more complex framework of Megaproject Social Responsibility (Ma et al., 2021; Zhou & Mi, 2017), as presented in Chapter 2 of this book.

Figure 4. Specific SDGs sub-targets covered in our analysis

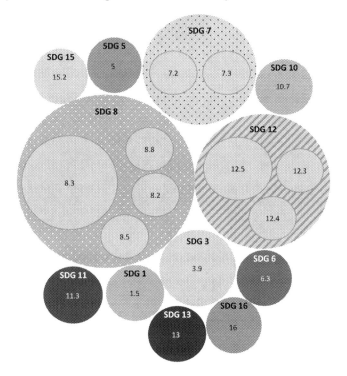

Source: authors' own elaboration on data retrieved from the sample processed by the SDG Mapper tool.

3.6. Summary

This chapter has explored the relationship between critical infrastructure (CI) and sustainable development, focusing on megaprojects in the transportation sector. CI are vital elements in a country's economy, providing essential services whose disruption could lead to significant societal problems. The research field on critical infrastructure and climate change is still in its early stages, but it is crucial for achieving the SDGs. Critical infrastructure plays a vital role in furthering various SDGs, such as clean energy, transportation, clean water, sanitation, and disaster management. The chapter presents a benchmark analysis of megaprojects in the transportation sector, analyzing their impacts on SDGs. The analysis found connections to 12 out of 17 SDGs, highlighting the paradoxical nature of critical infrastructure.

3.7. Annex I: list of impacts

ECONOMIC IMPACTS

1. Respecting the time and budget of the construction works of the infrastructure.
2. Job creation (direct and indirect) and attraction of local talent.
3. Economic impact on local companies.
4. Attraction of private capital.
5. Attraction of other European funding.
6. Reduction of economic disparities between the regions joined by the infrastructure.
7. Increase in services in the area where the infrastructure is placed.
8. Increase in tourist flows.
9. Development of new technologies and innovations during the infrastructure construction.
10. Indirect contribution to the local economy through the expenses of the workers and families located there.
11. Creation of jobs for local workers.
12. Creation of an innovation ecosystem around the sites (start-ups and spin-offs, collaboration with universities and polytechnics.
13. Improvement of local infrastructure quality and services.
14. Improvement of local economics in connecting different regions.
15. Sourcing food from local producers and retailers.
16. Economic stability of territories after the end of the construction works.
17. Support for business creation and entrepreneurship.
18. Direct local economy support through the involvement of local companies.

SOCIAL IMPACTS

1. Actions to minimize disruption to communities.
2. Reducing the time taken to transport goods and/or people.
3. Financing of training paths for the creation of technical and managerial skills among the local community.

4. Attention to gender-balanced job creation.
5. Multicultural company.
6. Facilitating sustainable urban travel.
7. Co-design with direct involvement of the local population.
8. Whistleblowing available to the local population (email) and SMS notification system for any inconvenience caused to citizens.
9. Recovery of food surpluses in the canteens of worksites and train workers in the right practiced for food waste avoidance.
10. Adoption of recruitment policies to support gender equality also among business partners in the yards.
11. Updating on the megaproject dedicated website of the state of the art, with webcams on construction sites.
12. On-site health care for non-resident personnel, so as not to clog up the local health structure.
13. Attraction of unemployed local human capital.
14. Preventive actions to reduce inconvenience to citizens, for safety around construction sites, and during the handling/transport of material, such as the construction of car parks (following the transfer of workers on site).
15. Collaboration with local training organizations to recruit local employees, investing in their education.
16. Construction of kindergarten as a result of the creation of a long-term building site, which will then be donated to the municipality.
17. Creation of business info points for citizenship.
18. Reduction of traffic congestion.
19. Provision of pre-employment training courses with local training organizations (welders, carpenters, pipe fitters).
20. Open-door events and site visits.
21. Events to disseminate the work with the territory for the co-creation of social measures, not fully financed, but co-designed.
22. Interventions to support children in marginalized communities
23. Establishment of Academy-style in-house training courses
24. Moments of dialogue with the local community
25. Number of beneficiaries of social impact projects implemented.
26. Number of working days lost due to sabotage or protest events by citizens.
27. Social impact projects co-created with the community.
28. Corporate volunteering projects with the community.
29. Recruitment of staff from vulnerable groups such as refugee engineers.
30. Availability of all public documents on the company website.
31. Reassignment and retraining of temporary workers hired for the construction works.

32. Restoration of archaeological sites following any finds.
33. Respect for different ethnicities, cultures, religions and beliefs in the workplace.
34. Development of public policies.
35. Increase in indiscriminate traffic due to the construction works.
36. Exploitation of foreign labor and concerns about human rights abuses.
37. Expropriations.

HEALTH AND SAFETY

1. Safety of the infrastructure and quality of the materials.
2. Environmental and health, safety and human rights audits of suppliers.
3. Accidents, fatalities and near misses in the workplace.
4. Accidents by workers on the home-work journey.
5. Promotion of a health and safety culture on construction sites (training)
6. Analysis of traffic and the impact of works on traffic in neighboring communities.
7. Number of accidents occurring in terms of traffic in the areas surrounding construction sites.
8. Health and safety training for direct and indirect workers.
9. Safety and control entrusted to robots for structural inspections, development, and use of innovations.
10. Increase in respiratory diseases as a result of increased traffic.

ENVIRONMENTAL IMPACTS

1. Impacts on quality of water, air, land, and biodiversity.
2. Contribution to climate change in terms of emissions.
3. Expected rainfall.
4. Circular economy from re-used excavation waste.
5. Circular economy from reused water.
6. Air dehumidification plants to prevent corrosion of materials.
7. Use of renewable energy and photovoltaics with consequent energy consumption.
8. Overall reduction of emissions thanks to the megaproject.
9. Minimizing environmental impact on fauna, flora and groundwater.
10. Compensatory environmental measures: clean air survey system, fish ladders, clean water technologies, bat houses, forest protection, orchid habitat, plants instead of concrete.
11. Transparent waste management during excavations.
12. Compensatory actions: tree planting, air purifiers, fish ladders, water purifiers, bat houses, protection of protected flora.

13. Circular utilization, reuse of abandoned areas within local communities for the period of the works, then return to the community.
14. Acoustic mitigation with replacement of windows in houses most exposed to noise pollution, especially for poor people.
15. Circular use of the extracted material for the production of spritz concrete.
16. Establishment of an environmental education observatory.
17. Management of asbestos.

References

Achillopoulou, D.V, Mitoulis, S.A., Argyroudis, S.A. & Wang, Y. (2020). Monitoring of transport infrastructure exposed to multiple hazards: A roadmap for building resilience. *Science of the Total Environment*, 746, 141001.

AIIC (Italian Association of Critical Infrastructures Experts) (2017). *Guidelines for Community Resilience Evaluation*. https://www.infrastrutture critiche.it/wp-content/uploads/2021/05/COMMUNITY_Resilience_AIIC.pdf.

Almeida, N., Trindade, M., Komljenovic, D. & Finger, M. (2022). A conceptual construct on value for infrastructure asset management. *Utilities Policy*, 75(April), 101354. https://doi.org/10.1016/j.jup.2022.101354.

Argyroudis, S.A., Mitoulis, S.A., Hofer, L., Zanini, M.A., Tubaldi, E. & Frangopol, D.M. (2020). Resilience assessment framework for critical infrastructure in a multi-hazard environment: Case study on transport assets. *Science of the Total Environment*, 714, 136854.

Boin, A. & McConnell, A. (2007). Preparing for critical infrastructure breakdowns: the limits of crisis management and the need for resilience. *Journal of Contingencies and Crisis Management*, 15(1), 50–59.

Boin, A. & Smith, D. (2006). Terrorism and critical infrastructures: Implications for public-private crisis management. *Public Money and Management*, 26(5), 295–304.

Brookes, N. & Elmahroug, M.H. (2015). *The Megaproject Portfolio*. University of Leeds.

Cao, X. & Lam, J.S.L. (2019). Catastrophe risk assessment framework of ports and industrial clusters: A case study of the Guangdong province. *International Journal of Shipping and Transport Logistics*, 11(1), 1–24.

Cedergren, A., Lidell, K. & Lidell, K. (2019). Critical infrastructures and the tragedy of the commons dilemma: Implications from institutional restructuring on reliability and safety. *Journal of Contingencies and Crisis Management*, 27(4), 282–292.

Coaffee, J. & Clarke, J. (2017). Critical infrastructure lifelines and the politics of anthropocentric resilience. *Resilience*, 5(3), 161–181.

De Bruijne, M., Van Eeten, M., Roe, E. & Schulman, P. (2006). Assuring high reliability of service provision in critical infrastructures. *International Journal of Critical Infrastructures*, 2(2–3), 231–246.

de Gooyert, V. (2020). Long term investments in critical infrastructure under environmental turbulence. Dilemmas of infrastructure responsiveness. *Sustainable Futures*, 2(April), 100028.

Egan, M.J. (2007). Anticipating future vulnerability: Defining characteristics of increasingly critical infrastructure-like systems. *Journal of Contingencies and Crisis Management*, 15(1), 4–17.

European Commission (2008). Council Directive 2008/114/EC on the identification and designation of European critical infrastructures and the assessment of the need to improve their protection.

Forzieri, G., Bianchi, A., Batista e Silva, F.B., Herrera, M.A.M., Leblois, A., Lavalle, C. & Feyen, L. (2018). Escalating impacts of climate extremes on critical infrastructures in Europe. *Global Environmental Change*, 48, 97–107.

Forzieri, G., Bianchi, A., Marin Herrera, M.A., Batista e Silva, F., Lavalle, C. & Feyen, L. (2016). *Resilience of large investments and critical infrastructures in Europe to climate change*. EUR27906; doi:10.2788/232049

Fritzon, Å., Ljungkvist, K., Boin, A. & Rhinard, M. (2007). Protecting Europe's critical infrastructures: Problems and prospects. *Journal of Contingencies and Crisis Management*, 15(1), 30–41.

Ghorbani, A.A. & Bagheri, E. (2008). The state of the art in critical infrastructure protection: a framework for convergence. *International Journal of Critical Infrastructures*, 4(3), 215–244.

Hallegatte, S., Green, C., Nicholls, R.J. & Corfee-Morlot, J. (2013). Future flood losses in major coastal cities. *Nature Climate Change*, 3(9), 802–806.

Intergovernmental Panel on Climate Change. (2022). *Climate Change 2022. Imapcts, Adaptation and Vulnerability*. Retrieved from https://www.ipcc.ch/report/ar6/wg2/downloads/report/IPCC_AR6_WGII_FinalDraft_FullReport.pdf.

Iturriza, M., Labaka, L., Sarriegi, J.M. & Hernantes, J. (2018). Modelling methodologies for analysing critical infrastructures. *Journal of Simulation*, 12(2), 128–143.

Jönsson, S. (2010). Interventionism – an approach for the future? *Qualitative Research in Accounting & Management*, 7(1), 124–134.

Kamran, M. (2022). Role of cultural heritage in promoting the resilience of linear/critical infrastructure system with the enhancement of economic dimension of resilience: a critical review. *International Journal of Construction Management*, 22(7), 1345–1354.

Knodt, M., Fraune, C. & Engel, A. (2021). Local governance of critical infrastructure resilience: Types of coordination in German cities. *Journal of Contingencies and Crisis Management*, (November), 1–10.

Kumar, N., Poonia, V., Gupta, B.B. & Goyal, M.K. (2021). A novel framework for risk assessment and resilience of critical infrastructure towards climate change. *Technological Forecasting and Social Change*, 165(April), 120532.

Liu, X., Fang, Y.-P. & Zio, E. (2021). A Hierarchical Resilience Enhancement Framework for Interdependent Critical Infrastructures. *Reliability Engineering & System Safety*, 215, 107868.

Ma, H., Sun, D., Zeng, S., Lin, H. & Shi, J.J. (2021). The Effects of Megaproject Social Responsibility on Participating Organizations. *Project Management Journal*, 52(5), 418–433.

Mikellidou, C.V., Shakou, L.M., Boustras, G. & Dimopoulos, C. (2018). Energy critical infrastructures at risk from climate change: A state of the art review. *Safety Science*, 110, 110–120.

OECD (2017), Investing in Climate, Investing in Growth, OECD Publishing.

OECD (2018). Climate-resilient Infrastructure. Policy Perspectives. *OECD Environment Policy Paper*, 14(14), 1–46.

Ouyang, M. (2014). Review on modeling and simulation of interdependent critical infrastructure systems. *Reliability Engineering & System Safety*, 121, 43–60.

Rehak, D., Senovsky, P., Hromada, M. & Lovecek, T. (2019). Complex approach to assessing resilience of critical infrastructure elements. *International Journal of Critical Infrastructure Protection*, 25, 125–138.

Rehak, D., Senovsky, P. & Slivkova, S. (2018). Resilience of critical infrastructure elements and its main factors. *Systems*, 6(2).

Schulman, P.R. & Roe, E. (2007). Designing infrastructures: Dilemmas of design and the reliability of critical infrastructures. *Journal of Contingencies and Crisis Management*, 15(1), 42–49.

Schulman, P., Roe, E., Van Eeten, M. & De Bruijne, M. (2015). High reliability and the management of critical infrastructures. *The Routledge Companion to Strategic Risk Management*, 12(1), 463–481.

Splichalova, A., Patrman, D., Kotalova, N. & Hromada, M. (2020). Managerial decision making in indicating a disruption of critical infrastructure element resilience. *Administrative Sciences*, 10(3).

Vallejo, L. & Mullan, M. (2017). *Climate-resilient infrastructure: Getting the Policies Right*. Environment Working Paper No. 121. OECD.

van den Adel, M.J., de Vries, T.A. & van Donk, D.P. (2022). Resilience in interorganizational networks: dealing with day-to-day disruptions in critical infrastructures. *Supply Chain Management*, 27(7), 64–78.

Wang, T., Xu, J., He, Q., Chan, A.P.C. & Owusu, E.K. (2022). Studies on the success criteria and critical success factors for mega infrastructure construction projects: a literature review. *Engineering, Construction and Architectural Management*.

Winch, Graham M. (2017). *Oxford Handbooks Online Megaproject Stakeholder Management*, (November), 1–27.

Zhou, Z. & Mi, C. (2017). Social responsibility research within the context of megaproject management: Trends, gaps and opportunities. *International Journal of Project Management*, 35(7), 1378–1390.

Zio, E. (2016a). Challenges in the vulnerability and risk analysis of critical infrastructures. *Reliability Engineering & System Safety*, 152, 137–150.

Zio, E. (2016b). Critical infrastructures vulnerability and risk analysis. *European Journal for Security Research*, 1(2), 97–114.

Chapter 4
A LITERATURE REVIEW ON IMPACT ACCOUNTING & STAKEHOLDER MANAGEMENT

ABSTRACT: *This chapter presents systematic literature review on previous studies on socio-economic and environmental impact accounting and discusses the main findings in terms of the state-of-the-art in accounting and reporting practices for megaprojects and sustainable infrastructure and missing topics. This chapter aims to look for and point out 1) the main authors, journals and countries contributing to megaprojects and sustainable infrastructure projects in the business and accounting area, 2) the main research area of accounting studies within the megaprojects and sustainable infrastructure field, and 3) the current research gaps and future research trends for accounting studies toward the development of a sustainable infrastructure projects' management. The literature review analyzed, adopting the PRISMA framework, 151 scientific contributions (out of 323 initial selected works) in the business subject area related to accounting practices for megaprojects. Cluster analysis on the keyword co-occurrence network revealed five main clusters including 1) project management, 2) governance, 3) decision-making, 4) economic and social impacts, and 5) risk assessment.*

SUMMARY: 4.1. Main features of megaprojects. – 4.1.1. Types of megaprojects. – 4.1.2. Projects' phases. – 4.1.3. Sustainable infrastructure's pillars. – 4.1.4. Impact accounting category. – 4.2. Methodology. – 4.2.1. Research questions. – 4.2.2. Protocol and research sample. – 4.2.3. Coding framework. – 4.3. Results. 4.3.1. Trend. – 4.3.2. Journal. – 4.3.3. Citation network. – 4.3.4. Geographic distribution. – 4.3.5. Topic trends. – 4.3.6. Keyword co-occurrence. – 4.4. Discussion. – 4.4.1. Future research trends. – 4.5. Summary. – *References.*

4.1. Main features of megaprojects

Megaprojects, typically defined as "*large-scale, complex ventures that typically cost US$1 billion or more, take many years to develop and build, involve multiple public and private stakeholders, are transformational, and impact millions of people*" (Flyvbjerg, 2014), include transportation infrastructure such as airports, high-speed railways (HSRs), or maritime ports (Flyvbjerg et al., 2003), large hydroelectric power stations or dams (Stone, 2008), as well as political projects such as the Apollo programme (Horwitch, 1990) or temporary events as the Olympic Games (Golubchikov, 2017; Shakirova, 2015). Due to their complexity, wide and long generated impacts, and the multitude of actors and stakeholders involved, generally they are considered as a *"system-of-systems"* (Thacker et al., 2019) and are affected by the so-called "uniqueness bias" (Flyvbjerg, 2014, p. 9). However, they are constantly increasing in investments (Ma et al., 2020).

Such a complexity cannot be untangled perfectly but in the past decades academics and scholars, practitioners and large international institutions such as the United Nations or the OECD attempted to clarify several of the fundamental aspects of megaproject management, proposing classification for the types of megaprojects and infrastructure, project phases as well as impact category areas. Such aspects will be briefly discussed in the following subsections and analyzed in detail in this chapter thanks to a systematic literature review.

4.1.1. Types of megaprojects

There is not a unique and exhaustive classification for megaprojects. With respect to physical infrastructure projects, for instance, Thacker et al. (2019) classified infrastructure into five main categories: energy, transport, water or waste management facilities and telecommunications. Although the majority of megaprojects refers to physical infrastructure, they should not be intended only as construction projects. Indeed, recalling the general definition of Sykes (1990), *megaprojects can include events such as the Olympic Games* (Randeree, 2014) *or the Universal Expo* (Shakirova, 2015), *redevelopment of urban setting* (Dogan & Stupar, 2017), *international infrastructural long-term policy projects, such as the Belt and Road Initiative (BRI)* (Daye et al., 2020)*, or even large aerospace programs such as the Apollo Programs of the United States* (Horwitch, 1990). The Sustainable Infrastructure Tool Navigator, developed in collaboration with the UN Environment Programme (UNEP), adopts a ten-sector classification (German Cooperation and UNEP, 2022) – urban planning, waste, ICT/digital, natural infrastructure, water and sanitation, buildings, energy, food systems, transportation, and health – including also, among others, natural infrastructure. The OECD (2019) simply refers to energy, transport and a general sector. *Since there is not a unique classification and too detailed groups can create confusion (many scientific contributions do not refer to a specific type of infrastructure), in this work we have adopted a five-type classification starting from the three groups proposed by the* OECD (2019) and including temporary events and urban/rural planning and policy: energy, transportation, temporary events, urban/rural planning and general construction infrastructure.

4.1.2. Projects' phases

Similarly, the execution of a megaproject is based on several life cycle phases, starting from the earlier planning or design phases to the construction, until the use or the decommissioning phases. As for the type of infrastructure, there is also not a unique classification for the project phases within the scientific literature, although there exist recognized protocols that define the fundamental phases for project management. The Project Management Institute (2017, pp. 49–51) includes four phases – starting the project, organizing and preparing, carrying out the work, ending the project – that can be split into several other sub-phases such as concept development, feasibility study, customer requirements, design, prototype, build, test and so on. Generally, the project life cycle phases are sub-sequential and between each pair of phases there are decision gates, but what the main phases of a project are is not unambiguously defined. For instance, Zidane et al. (2016) proposed 8 phases,[1] while Priemus (2010) only five.[2] The OECD (2019) uses a framework with seven different and subsequent phases, starting from earlier strategic phase until the operation – prioritization, planning/preparation, procurement, detailed design, finance, construction, operation/maintenance – while the Sustainable Infrastructure Tool Navigator is based on a eleven-phase classification, from an initial "enabling environment", until the "decommissioning/repurposing" (German Cooperation and UNEP, 2022). In this work, we adopted a simpler classification due the difficulty to homogenize all the different classifications by aggregating the initial phases (the ones that have more differences among the academic works) into a single and generic one: front-end, construction, operation, End of Life.

4.1.3. Sustainable infrastructure's pillars

With respect to impacts generated and to the fundamental pillars of sustainable infrastructure, although small differences among frameworks exist, in this case the general aspects for an evaluation framework are quite similar. Indeed, starting from the well-known 3E framework – environment, economy, equity – the United Nations (UN) Commission for Sustainable Development (United Nations, 2001) proposed four areas, by adding the

---

[1] Identification, conception, front-end, plan and design, construction, closeout, operation, and procurement.

[2] Problem analysis, programme of requirements, elaboration of the technical aspects, realization, and operation after completion.

institutional area (see Chapter 1). Similarly, the Inter-American Development Bank (2018) proposed the same four areas (and 14 sub-aspects and more than 60 criteria and indicators) as a general framework for sustainable infrastructure. In this work, due to some blurriness and differences in the definition of the institutional area we simply rely on the worldwide recognized three sustainability pillars, i.e., economy, environment and equity.

4.1.4. Impact accounting category

Finally, as previously mentioned, megaprojects impact, positively or negatively, on large territories and local populations both in the short, medium and long-term. Hence, accounting research works, in the past years, focused on the different stages of a social and environmental impact evaluation, from stakeholder engagement and management (Derakhshan et al., 2019) to the identification and evaluation of impact categories (Lin et al., 2017), until the reporting for strategic management (Barrett, 1979; Gosasang et al., 2018). The evaluation of the impacts generated by megaprojects gained its momentum especially in the last decade, with the increasing interest in sustainable infrastructure and their development. Indeed, the recent call for intergenerational justice moved the focus from earlier studies on projects' performance, traditionally intended as the delivery of a project on time and without cost overrunning (Fahri et al., 2015), to the development of sustainable infrastructure systems. Indeed, ranking systems, such as the Envision rating system, have been recently introduced properly to evaluate the sustainability of infrastructure, considering aspects from the quality of life to the resource allocation or climate and risk (McWhirter & Shealy, 2018). Thus, the evaluation of megaprojects' impacts should include both internal, i.e., on project performance and deliverable (Caldas & Gupta, 2017), and external impacts, i.e., on local communities, primary and secondary stakeholders, as well as on the environment (Lin et al., 2017; Nourelfath et al., 2022).

In this sense, the aim of impact accounting in megaprojects is twofold. On one hand, understanding, evaluating and reporting the generated impacts, both internal and external, is crucial to improve project performance and the rate of success of megaprojects (Caldas & Gupta, 2017). Hence, improving the transparency and trust can support the management of internal and external stakeholders and can prevent the emergence of conflicts and disputes (Cerić et al., 2021; Wang et al., 2020). On the other side, impact accounting is the foundation of risk assessment and of forecasting unpredictable future events (Li et al., 2018), thus, a fundamental requirement for strategic planning (van Dijk, 2021). Planning is not to be intended simply as 'knowing and controlling' (p. 3), rather as evaluating and forecasting impacts, both predictable and unpredictable, to support megaprojects' management both at operational, tactical and strategic level (Zidane et al., 2016). In this sense, it is crucial to distinguish among short, mid and long-term impacts, and between outputs and outcomes. According to Zidane et al. (2016), the output of a project is the "product" itself (e.g. a new rail line or an airport), while the outcome should be intended as the result of the output (new passengers can move from one city to another one) and the impacts as the satisfied need (creation of new jobs, decrease of CO_2 emissions). Impacts can be both positive or negative. For instance, during the construction phase of a megaproject, thousands of new jobs can be created (positive impact) but the environment can be devastated or CO_2 emissions can increase (negative impact). Clearly, each impact affects different stakeholders. Land and environment exploitation affects local communities, while the provided service (e.g. a new high-velocity rail line) may be used by citizens from different countries, economic benefits can refer to private industries, contractors and local employees.

Concluding, there is not a globally recognized classification of the phases of an accounting process. Generally, it starts from the identification and prioritization of the affected stakeholders (boundary conditions), it follows with the mapping of the outcomes and the evaluation of the corresponding impacts and it ends with the reporting of the evaluated impacts. In this sense, although highly criticized (Maldonado & Corbey, 2016), the Social Return on Investment (SROI) framework provides a useful guide to the different stages. Nicholls et al. (2012) defines six stages of a SROI analysis: 1) establishing scope and identifying stakeholders, 2) mapping outcomes, 3) evidencing outcomes and giving them a value, 4) establishing impact, 5) calculating the SROI, 6) reporting, using and embedding. Aware of the current critics emerging from literature about economically evaluating environmental and social impacts, in this work we adopt the six stages as a coding and interpretative framework for the different tasks of impact accounting.

4.2. Methodology

This chapter aims at evaluating the role and contribution of management studies, in particular the accounting field, for the advancement of megaprojects and sustainable infrastructure through a systematic literature review (SLR) method (Massaro et al., 2016). SLR permits to qualitatively and quantitatively assess and analyze a large corpus of scientific literature allowing the replicability of the methodology and of the findings. Moreover, bibliometric analyses support the identification of the most important journals, authors, papers and topics and their consequent ranking (Paul & Criado,

2020; Dal Mas et al., 2019). Typically, a SLR relies on a few main general methodological steps (Massaro et al., 2016): 1) define the research questions, 2) specify the research protocol and methodology, 3) define the corpus of literature, 4) choose an analytical framework for coding and analyze data with the developed framework, 5) discuss findings. First, together with the research questions, the type of study as well as the rationale and scope of the study must be defined. Second, a reliable methodology must be chosen in order to be easily replicable, such as the PRISMA methodology (Liberati et al., 2009; Moher et al., 2010). Third, a proper coding framework has to be identified and used to analyze the literature corpus. Finally, a critical discussion aimed at answering the defined research questions and at identifying current research gaps and consequent future research topics (Dumay et al., 2016).

4.2.1. Research questions

This work aims at answering a few research questions to untangle the complexity related to megaprojects' and sustainable infrastructure projects' management and to clarify the state-of-arts and the past research trends, as well as to point out most important authors, journals and topics. Thus, the following research questions are addressed:

RQ0: what are the main authors, journals and countries contributing to megaprojects and sustainable infrastructure projects in the business and accounting area?

RQ1: what are the main research areas of accounting studies within the megaprojects and sustainable infrastructure field?

RQ2: what are the current research gaps and future research trends for accounting studies toward the development of a sustainable infrastructure projects' management?

4.2.2. Protocol and research sample

This literature review is based on the PRISMA (Preferred Reporting Items for Systematic reviews and Meta-Analyses) framework (Liberati et al., 2009; Moher et al., 2010). The analyzed corpus of literature corresponds to the set of scientific contributions (articles, in-proceedings, working papers, book chapters) obtained through the query *"SUBJAREA(busi) TITLE-ABS-KEY(("sustainable infrastructure*" OR "megaproject*" OR "mega project*" OR "mega-project*" OR "mega infrastructure*" OR "major project*") AND (environment* OR social* OR economic* OR sustainab*) AND (impact* OR* *assess* OR account* OR report* OR output* OR outcome*))"* on the Scopus database, being aware of the limitations related by excluding other databases for scientific publications. The query was built in order to identify contributions related to megaprojects and sustainable infrastructure (and synonyms) related to the evaluation, assessing, and reporting of social, economic and environmental impacts. The rationale was to filter the results on megaprojects and sustainable infrastructure with respect to the three pillars of sustainability (environmental, economic, and social, including a generic "sustainab*" term) and terms related to the Social Return On Investment (SROI) approach (Nicholls et al., 2012), i.e., impact* OR assess* OR account* OR report* OR output* OR outcome*. Only contributions in English have been considered, while non article contributions were included only for the first step of the analysis, without analyzing them through the coding framework. The query was run on 2 June 2022.

Figure 1. Flowchart of the selection process for the considered contributions

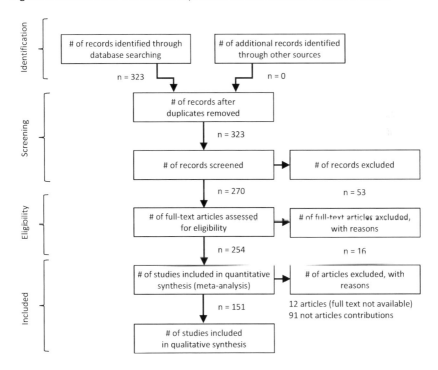

Source: authors' own elaboration.

According to the PRISMA framework, Figure 1 shows the four steps – Identification, Screening, Eligibility, Included - of the selection process from the initial query to the # of studies included in the qualitative synthesis and the # of studies included in quantitative synthesis. The total number of contributions from the query was 323 documents (212 articles, 111 other contributions). After a first round of screening based on the titles, keywords and abstracts 53 contributions not related to megaprojects (e.g. small buildings) or to impact accounting (in its broadest sense, i.e., internal impacts on project performance or external impacts on stakeholders and environment) have been removed. Consequently, the subset of articles has been deeply analyzed by reading the full article-texts by excluding other 16 articles, not relevant or for those that were not possible to download the full article text (12 articles). The authors, aware of the blurriness between megaprojects and sustainable infrastructure, in the literature also intended as small sustainable buildings, have adopted the following general criteria for eligibility. First, contributions about small infrastructure projects such as buildings and family houses have been discarded; second, contributions related to the Envision framework for sustainable infrastructure have been included even if not directly applied to megaprojects, because currently Envision is the only standard widely applied to megaprojects. Similarly, contributions about the general assessment framework for sustainable infrastructure have been included. Finally, since urban, or rural, planning projects have a long-term impact and generally consist of policies for hundreds of million euros, contributions related to urban planning, cities or large redevelopment policies have been included too. Urban and rural planning can include redevelopment strategies for cities after mega-events (Golubchikov, 2017) as well as infrastructural territorialization policies as the Russian strategy for the development of the Arctic area (Leksin & Porfiryev, 2015). Consequently, the whole dataset was analyzed through the R package bibliometrix (Aria & Cuccurullo, 2017) considering both articles and not articles. We decided to include both articles and not article contributions because the literature related to megaprojects is varied and interdisciplinary by nature and book chapters, books and conference proceedings represent a fundamental part of the scientific literature; thus, it is crucial for the understanding of current trends and topics. On the contrary, due to the difficulty of finding the full texts of all non-article contributions, they have been excluded for the second step of the analysis. Thus, only the subset corresponding to the articles was coded and deeply analyzed according to the criteria described in the following paragraph.

4.2.3. Coding framework

The selected subset, composed by both articles and non-article contributions was analyzed and described with respect to: general trend, journal impact, citation network, geographic distribution, topics' trend, and co-occurrence keyword network. Moreover, the final subset of selected articles was classified based on a few criteria:

- Case study: yes/no.
- Sustainability area: social, economic, environmental.
- Project types: energy, transportation, temporary events, urban/rural planning and general construction infrastructure.
- Project phase: front-end, construction, operation, End of Life.
- Evaluation stage: stage 1, establishing scope and identifying stakeholders; stage 2, mapping outcomes; stage 3, demonstrating outcomes and giving them a value; stage 4, establishing impact; stage 5, calculating the SROI; stage 6, reporting, using and embedding.
- Topic: project management, governance, decision-making, social, economic and environmental impacts, and risk assessment.

The topic was selected by analyzing the clusters identified thanks to the Louvain clustering algorithm (De Meo et al., 2011) applied to the co-occurrence network based on keyword plus (authors' keyword plus self-generated Scopus keywords). The evaluation stages correspond to the subsequent stages of a SROI analysis (Nicholls et al., 2012) and have been used to highlight if a contribution was mainly focused on identifying the affected stakeholders, prioritizing or evaluating the generated impacts or on the final reporting/dissemination. For instance, a contribution focused on analyzing stakeholders relationships belongs to stage 1, a framework for indicators to stage 4 or the social cost of carbon (SCOC) to stage 5. In particular, stage 3 and stage 5 refer to contributions that attempt to evaluate the cost of the impacts (therefore not directly related to SROI).

4.3. Results

Findings are presented in two subsequent sections. First, a descriptive analysis and meta-analysis of the corpus of literature is presented by focusing on the yearly trends of the number of contributions, top journals and keywords, as well as on the co-citation network (to point out top authors), and worldwide collaborations. Second, from the analysis of the topics' trends and the co-occurrence keyword network five main topics have been identified and used to discuss in detail the subset of corpus related to the scientific articles.

4.3.1. Trend

Figure 2 shows the increasing trend of the scientific contributions related to megaprojects, major projects and sustainable infrastructure in the business area. Although the first contributions can be dated back to the end of the 1970s, the interest in megaproject management started with some precursory articles in the early 1990s. However, only in the last decade the topic got a lot of attention from the academic community, passing from a few contributions per year to more than 20 contributions per year after 2014. This trend is mainly due to the increasing interest in sustainable infrastructure and the consequent analysis of environmental, social and economic impacts.

Figure 2. Number of contributions per year related to megaprojects and sustainable infrastructure in the business area

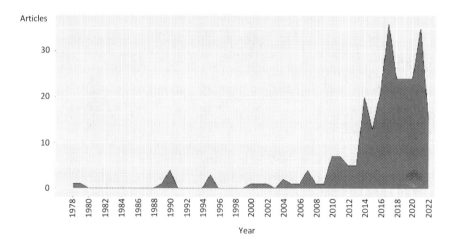

Source: authors' own elaboration.

4.3.2. Journal

Figure 3 exhibits the trend of the contributions per year per source (journals and conferences). The top journal since the 1990s is undoubtedly the International Journal of Project Management, which shows an exponential increase in the last 10-15 years. Other relevant journals are the Journal of Cleaner Production, Engineering, Construction and Architectural Management journal, the Journal of Construction Engineering and Management, the Journal of Management in Engineering and the Project Management Journal. The majority of contributions are dominated by engineering studies, followed by applied management journals. The topic of megaprojects' and sustainable infrastructures' management got its momentum since 2014 thanks to a few international conferences about sustainable infrastructure and accounting protocols such as the Envision rating system, officially launched during the International Conference on Sustainable Infrastructure (ICSI) in 2014. Nowadays, therefore, the presence of scientific contributions in accounting journals is still very limited.

Figure 3. Number of contributions per year for different sources (scientific journals and conferences)

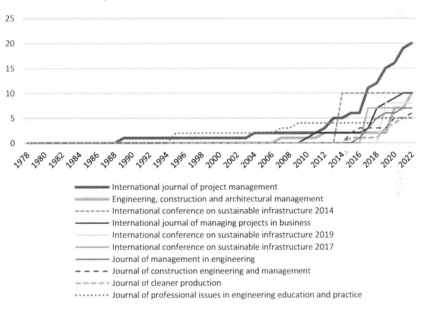

Source: authors' own elaboration.

4.3.3. Citation network

Figure 4 shows the co-citation network. The top and central author is clearly Bent Flyvbjerg, Professor and Chair at University of Oxford, with his seminal paper "*What you should know about megaprojects and why: an overview*" (Flyvbjerg, 2014). Figure 4, moreover shows four different clusters of contributions. The red and blue clusters are two general clusters with international collaborations among the UK, US, Australia and China. The green cluster is mainly focused on UK/Europe and China collaborations around nuclear power plants decommissioning, while the violet cluster is basically composed by Chinese contributions and authors. From Fig. 4, thus, emerges that the most interrelated countries are the UK, China, Australia and USA.

Figure 4. Co-citation network of scientific contributions for megaprojects and sustainable infrastructure in the business area

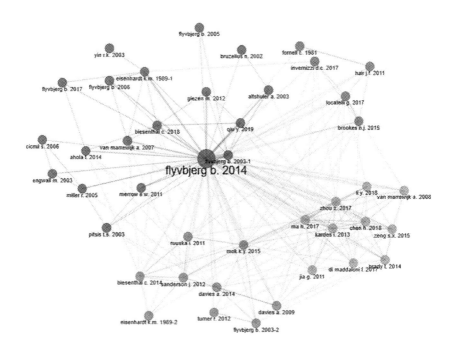

Source: authors' own elaboration.

4.3.4. Geographic distribution

Figure 5 presents the geographic distributions and international collaborations among countries. The top four countries are the United States of America (USA), United Kingdom (UK), People's Republic of China (PRC) and Australia. In addition, many contributions come from authors distributed worldwide, although the top contributors are from Europe, North America, Brazil and India. The top contributing universities in the top 4 countries are Shanghai University, the University of Leeds and Manchester, Harvard University and the University of Sydney and Melbourne. There is not a well-defined boundary on the topic distribution among different countries. However, the UK's distinguishing feature is related to contributions about nuclear decommissioning, while China's contribution is more connected to the developing of holistic frameworks for indicators (e.g. the literature on megaproject social responsibility), critical success factors and project performances due to the long-term experience on megaprojects. Finally, USA's contributions derive from a variety of topics, but the Envision rating system assumed an important space.

In the next subsections, the top keywords and topic trends are described in detail to point out the main research topics related to megaproject and sustainable infrastructure studies in the business area. All the graphs within the next sections refer to keywords plus, i.e., the authors' keywords plus the automatically generated keywords from Scopus. In all the graphs, the word megaproject and its synonyms (megaproject; megaprojects; mega project; mega projects) have been removed.

Figure 5. Collaboration among countries and geographic distribution of scientific contributions related to megaprojects and sustainable infrastructure in the business area

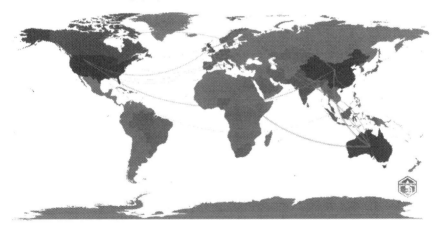

Source: authors' own elaboration.

4.3.5. Topic trends

Finally, Figures 6 and 7 show, respectively, the cumulative occurrences of the top 10 keywords per year and the wordcloud of the top 50 keywords within the whole dataset. The top keyword and topic is project management that exhibits an exponential growth in the last two decades, followed by sustainable development and sustainable infrastructure that gained a lot of interest from 2014, mainly due to the three International Conference on Sustainable Infrastructure held in 2014, 2017 and 2019. Other relevant keywords with an increasing trend in the last decade are Decision Making, Risk Assessment, Construction Industry, Risk Management, Infrastructure Project, and Economic and Social Effects.

Figure 6. Cumulative occurrence of keywords from the selected corpus of literature

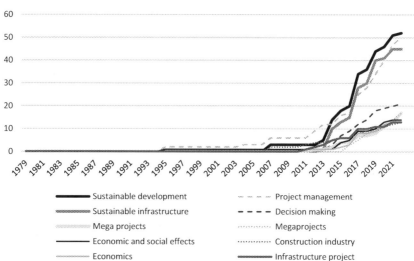

Source: authors' own elaboration.

Figure 7. Wordcloud of top keywords within the corpus of literature

Source: authors' own elaboration.

Figure 7 shows the wordcloud where the top keywords are respectively, decision making, risk assessment, risk management, construction industry and infrastructure project, as well as economic and social effects, investments and stakeholder. From the wordcloud, other relevant keywords emerged related to the type of infrastructure (bridges, transportation, architectural design, construction and engineering, urban planning), the methodology (structural equation modeling, literature reviews, least squares approximations, surveys, behavioral research) or the analyzed subtopics (social responsibilities, sustainability, governance approach, stakeholder management, contractors, innovation). Figures 6 and 7 confirm the necessity to analyze studies related to megaprojects with a holistic vision and that studies in the business area are contributing from a multitude of approaches and practices to the development of sustainable infrastructure and megaprojects.

Finally, Figure 8 shows the historical trend of top keywords and as they evolved during years. What emerges from the graph is a change in the focus and object of the studies during the last years. In particular, the earliest studies focused mainly on project management, risk assessment and construction industry (period 1978–2013) while from 2014 a shift occurred toward topics related to sustainability and sustainable development, economic and social effects and life cycle, as well as toward decision making and complexity. This confirms that the scientific literature moved from technical aspects to embrace a more holistic vision.

Figure 8. Thematic evolution of top keywords from 1978 to 2022 of studies in the business area related to megaprojects and sustainable infrastructure

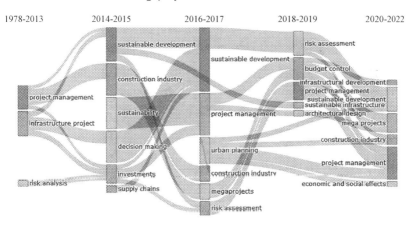

Source: authors' own elaboration.

Although project management remains the top keyword, Figure 8 highlights relevant aspects especially focusing on the sustainability and the generated impacts (typically the cause of conflicts, delays and failure), which explain the necessity to analyze deeper the decision-making and stakeholder management processes to address the challenge of megaproject complexity.

4.3.6. Keyword co-occurrence

Concluding this first descriptive analysis, Figure 9 represents the co-occurrence network of keywords. Five clusters of keywords emerge: sustainable development and decision making, governance approach, project management, risk assessment and economic and social effects/social responsibility. Moreover, various sub-topics for each cluster can be also highlighted. For instance, the project management cluster is more related to the complexity and performance of megaprojects, as well as to stakeholder management and conflict resolution. The governance cluster refers to topics such as infrastructural development, urban planning and tourism development. The decision-making cluster deals with decision making processes, life cycle and supply chain analysis, as well as to investments and budget control. Finally, the risk assessment and the social responsibility clusters are mainly focused on economic and social impacts and on their evaluation through different methodologies.

Figure 9. Keyword co-occurrence network

Source: authors' own elaboration.

4.4. Discussion

A total of 151 papers have been selected for the critical discussion of the research topics as shown in Figure 1. All the scientific contributions have been classified according to five aspects, i.e., topic treated, type of infrastructure, phase of the project, stage of evaluation and impact category. In particular, the topics correspond to the clusters described in Figure 9, the choice for the type of infrastructure, the phase of the project, the impact category and the evaluation stages have been detailed in the "background" section. Some articles are double-counted (e.g., an article can belong to project management and to decision making topic at the same time). The social impact category, i.e., equity, refers to articles that include the management of stakeholders or any type of analysis related to relationships among actors; thus, it does not refer only to the generated social impacts of a megaproject.

Table 1. Classification of the corpus of literature (only articles) into Topic, Type of infrastructure, Phase, Evaluation and Impact

Topic		Type		Phase		Evaluation		Impact	
Category	#	Category	#	Category	#	Category	#	Category	#
Project management	90	Energy	16	Front-end	56	Stage 1	64	Equity	106
Governance	30	Transport	36	Construction	101	Stage 2	51	Environment	56
Decision making	17	Events	5	Use	41	Stage 3	2	Economy	81
Economic and social impacts	31	Planning	8	EoL	23	Stage 4	11		
Risk assessment	13	General	83			Stage 5	9		
						Stage 6	2		

Source: authors' own elaboration.

Table 1 reports the summary after the classification of all the selected articles. In particular, although the majority of contributions still refers to project management, there is an increasing corpus of literature that focuses on the governance and on the economic and social impacts. With respect to the type of infrastructure, all physical infrastructure sectors are considered (energy, transport and construction), while mega-events or urban and rural planning projects are the least studied. On the contrary, referring to the project's phases, the majority focuses on the initial front-end and construction phases, while only a minor percentage considers the use and the End of Life phases. Typically the use and the End of Life phases are studied together with the construction phase and not as a uniquely objective. Finally, with respect to the evaluation stages, the majority of the contributions focused on the identification of stakeholders and their relationships, the establishment of generated outcomes and impacts, while only a few tried to compare environmental or social impacts to economic costs or analyzed the reporting stage.

Project management studies are mainly focused on complexity, stakeholder management, conflict resolution, and on technical contractual aspects. Since the earlier articles in the 1970s, studies related to project management represent the largest set of the literature, addressing a multitude of topics from traditional studies on stakeholder management (Chi et al., 2022; Mostafa & El-Gohary, 2015; Whitty & Maylor, 2009) to the analysis of the types of contracts (Griffiths, 1989; Lenferink et al., 2013; L. Ma & Fu, 2022; von Branconi & Loch, 2004) and public-private partnerships (Agarchand & Laishram, 2017; Kumaraswamy et al., 2007; Little, 2011; M. Wessels, 2014). Other studies addressed the issues of project performance (Di Maddaloni & Davis, 2017; Hu et al., 2012) and critical success factors (Caldas & Gupta, 2017; Fahri et al., 2015; Giezen, 2012; Hu et al., 2012; Kardes et al., 2013; Lopez del Puerto & Shane, 2014; J.R. Turner & Xue, 2018), complexity (Giezen, 2012; Kardes et al., 2013; Nyarirangwe & Babatunde, 2019; Y. Qiu et al., 2019) and conflict management, both among internal or primary stakeholders and external or secondary ones (Adityanandana & Gerber, 2019; Chang, 2013; Jia et al., 2011; Lee et al., 2017; Teo & Loosemore, 2010; van Marrewijk et al., 2016). Finally, a few studies addressed other topics such as trust (Anita Cerić et al., 2021; D. Wang et al., 2020), counter-accounting and NGO roles (Hamman, 2016), knowledge transfer (Mainga, 2017) and value creation (Chi et al., 2022; D.C. Invernizzi et al., 2019), and innovation (Badi et al., 2020; Chen et al., 2021; Liu & Ma, 2020) mechanisms. What emerged from the literature in project management topic is that there are several interrelated aspects that overpassed project management boundaries, strictly speaking, and shifted the focus to governance and decision-making approaches, social and economic impacts and risk assessment.

Governance plays a fundamental role for megaprojects for a variety of reasons, from approaches on how to manage stakeholders (Derakhshan et al., 2019) or strategies toward sustainability (Brunet & Aubry, 2018; Roelich et al., 2015; Maarten Wessels, 2014) to more long-term effects on territory. More precisely, since megaprojects can shape large territories for decades, the governance of megaprojects is essential especially in infrastructural territorialization strategies (Daye et al., 2020; Erie & MacKenzie, 2010; Golubchikov, 2017; Leksin & Porfiryev, 2015; Rocha & Neves, 2018), tourism development (Bowerman, 2021; Kanwal et al., 2020; Rehman et al., 2020; Shakirova, 2015) or urban planning (Dogan & Stupar, 2017; Y. Li et al., 2019; Sroka, 2021; Zheng, 2020). Currently, there are still many aspects underdeveloped in the literature, from the functioning of non-monetary transactions to the critical factors to maintain successful relations with the society, until the influence of external stakeholders to decision-making processes.

From the literature on decision-making processes, various sub-topics emerged such as sustainable development, life cycle and supply chain analysis or budget and investment control. There are various approaches that can be applied for decision-making processes: from participatory multicriteria decision analysis (MCDA) (Wei et al., 2016) to rating systems, such as the Envision rating system, a recent growing topic (McWhirter & Shealy, 2018; T. Shealy & Klotz, 2015; Tripp Shealy et al., 2016), from the evaluation of embodied impacts or life cycle analysis (Zeng et al., 2021) to Cost-Benefit analysis (CBA) (Litman & Brenman, 2012). All methodological approaches, then, support three levels of decision-making: 1) the technical level regards the project execution and deliverable, 2) the strategic level refers to the management of external disruptive factors, as environmental disruption, and 3) the institutional level focuses on the relationships between the context and the management and how they shape themselves reciprocally (Morris & Geraldi, 2011). Hence, decision-making is related to economic and social impacts and risk assessment and accounting practices become crucial to make the proper choices in complex environments.

The impacts generated by megaprojects is probably one of the earliest studied topics (Barrett, 1979; Connor-Lajambe, 1990; McCoy & Singer, 1978; Sabin, 1995), although still largely to be explored. The first research papers on impacts targeted both social, cultural (McCoy & Singer, 1978) and environmental aspects (Barrett, 1979). For instance McCoy & Singer (1978) developed a socio-cultural characteristic matrix, while the environmental counterpart was firstly developed in the 1970s in the UK and USA, initially introduced by BP and British Gas Corporation and later adopted by the National Environmental Policy Act (NEPA) in 1970 (Barrett, 1979). Although such statements were introduced in the 1970s, the impact evaluation tasks remained very inaccurate due to the complexity of megaprojects (Connor-Lajambe, 1990; Sabin, 1995). Both precise assessment methodologies (Nourelfath et al., 2022) and indicators systems (Lin et al., 2017) have been developed, while a holistic vision of megaprojects' impacts emerged mainly thanks to the introduction of Megaproject Social Responsibility (MSR) (Hanyang Ma et al., 2020) and the corresponding development of indicators' systems and evaluation framework (Lin et al., 2017).

Finally, accounting practices of the economic, social and environmental impacts cannot be seen only as an ex-post activity. Ex-ante evaluations are necessary for long-term strategic planning but not sufficient. In this perspective, risk assessment based on potential impacts can support decision-making processes, project management and the governance itself by taking into account uncertainties and risks. Recalling the work of Kardes et al. (2013), uncertainties in megaprojects are very common due to the high complexity of all megaprojects, and consequently should be predicted, faced or mitigated (when possible) through a proper decision-making process. In terms of social and environmental risks, for instance, Dyer (2017) identified social responsibility as a risk mitigation strategy when run through a cultural sense-making process. Indeed, understanding the social and cultural context of engaged local stakeholders can improve risk management and reduce the occurrence of conflictual events by improving the project performance and success as shown by Sandhu & Khan (2017).

4.4.1. Future research trends

From the literature five macro areas emerged: project management, governance, decision-making, social and economic effects, and risk assessment. Nowadays, most studies about megaprojects still lie in the project management field. Each topic is highly interconnected with the other ones and it cannot completely be analyzed and reported independently. Indeed, if on one side project management is related to managerial skills, critical success factors, adaptive behaviors of managers and to deliver a project on time without cost overrunning, the megaprojects' success and performance are deeply affected by external factors that cannot be managed with traditional project management strategies. Stakeholders have to be engaged in every phase of the project, especially in earlier ones (i.e. the planning or design phase), decision-making processes, and the governance itself, should be participatory, democratic and inclusive in order to avoid possible future risks of conflicts and disputes. Similarly, the accounting of social, environmental and economic impacts cannot only be seen as an ex-post evaluation. It is fundamental in the earlier phases to predict possible risks and unexpected events. On top of these considerations, several research gaps related to accounting studies emerged from this study.

First, the majority of studies includes the front-end phase (planning and design) and the construction phase, while the use/operation and the end of life phases (especially the EoL phase) are rarely taken into account. The use phase is normally considered in project management, in particular regarding contractual agreements between public and private parties such as, among others, the novel contracts Design-Build-Finance-Maintain (DBFM), Design-Build-Finance-Maintain-Operate (DBFMO), and their United States counterpart, Design-Build-Finance-Operate (DBFO), Build-Operate-Transfer (BOT) and Build-Own-Operate-Transfer (BOOT) (Lenferink et al., 2013). Generally, the use phase is considered at a strategic planning level (Y.J.T. Zidane et al., 2016). Studies including the EoL phase instead are limited in number and topics. The few studies addressing the EoL phase refer mainly to the decommissioning of nuclear power plants in UK (D.C. Invernizzi et al., 2019; Mulholland et al., 2020), the post-use of infrastructure built during mega-events (Golubchikov, 2017; Randeree, 2014) or in urban planning projects (Jain & Rohracher, 2022). In any case, the post-use and EoL phases are never studied quantitatively in terms of generated impacts. Similarly, although there is a large corpus of literature related to the critical success factors (mainly related to project management) during the planning, design and construction phases (Lopez del Puerto & Shane, 2014; Cepeda et al., 2018; Giezen, 2012; Caldas & Gupta, 2017), a few studies addressed CSFs during the use, post-use and EoL phases (J.R. Turner & Xue, 2018; Fahri et al., 2015).

Second, with respect to the type of evaluation – i.e. stage 1 to 6, from the analysis of stakeholder to the evaluation of the outcome or the reporting of the impacts – the majority of the work refers to the first stages. Indeed, while most past works focus on stage 1 (establishing scope and identifying stakeholders) and stage 2 (mapping outcomes), preferring qualitative case studies or theoretical analysis, only a few quantitatively evaluate the impacts (stage 4 and 5). In general, stage 3 of SROI analysis (demonstrating outcome and giving them a value) is not properly developed by past literature. In other words, although various works attempted to include different impacts (from displaced families to workers safety, from the impact on tourism to housing price), only a few translated the generated impacts in economic and financial terms (Hidayatno et al., 2015; Kim, 2010). In this sense, the majority of these studies belong to the sub-topic of risk assessment. Finally, there is a lack of studies focused on the final stage of a SROI analysis (stage 6: reporting, using and embedding). Although, the reporting stage, and the importance of communication strategies, were already considered as a crucial aspect for megaprojects within the Environmental Impact Statements (EISs) adopted by NEPA in the US in 1970 (Barrett, 1979), the current literature does not deeply study such aspect in relation with megaprojects. Only recently, China adopted a Social Stability Risk Assessment identifying communication as a fundamental axis to avoid social conflicts (Liu et al., 2016). In this sense, as seen earlier in the book, an emergent topic that is gaining its momentum in accounting literature is related to MSR (Ma et al., 2020; Zhou & Mi, 2017), i.e. a novel holistic vision that includes stakeholder engagement practices, the accounting of impacts and the consequent reporting. Notwithstanding the understanding of how reporting can affect, positively or negatively, megaproject performance is still at its infancy.

Finally, other secondary relevant gaps emerged from the literature review. The sub-branch related to the Envision rating system deeply analyzed the efficacy of the novel rating system in terms of supporting decision-makers. However, due to its novelty, currently there are no studies evaluating and comparing the real generated impacts after the construction with the score obtained by an infrastructure through the Envision rating system. In terms of novel approaches, instead, almost all studies identified bottom-up decision-making processes, stakeholder engagement activities as well as democratic and participatory governance as an essential aspect for megaproject success. However, most works see these inclusive activities as a managerial tool for project manager success, instead of addressing the will and needs of the secondary stakeholders. In this sense, some relevant studies, mainly related to urban setting and tourism development, proposed novel insights for megaproject management such as decentralized urban infrastructure development (Särkilahti et al., 2017) or inclusive governance to stimulate regenerative tourism strategies (Camargo & Vázquez-Maguirre, 2021). However, studies looking at decentralized megaproject development are still underexplored.

Last but not least, novel methodologies are appearing in the literature to face the still unavoidable forecasting errors of the generated impacts. Indeed, due to the complexity of megaprojects, it is necessary to analyze megaprojects as complex systems, thus adopting proper methodological tools. In this sense, some authors adopted system dynamics and system thinking to untangle the hidden causal relationships among factors, actors, and impacts (Cristiano & Gonella, 2019; Destyanto et al., 2017), but the literature in this sense is still to be explored. Table 2 shows a summary of future research trends starting from the identified gaps.

Table 2. Summary of future research trends per main topic area

Research topic area	Feature	Future trends
Project management	End of life contracts	What are the possible proper contracts for the dismantling and/or renovation of megaprojects?
	End of life impact in strategic planning	How can the End of Life impacts be taken into account in project management and in strategic planning of megaprojects?
	Critical success factors of use/ EoL phase	What are the critical success factors during the operation and dismantling phase?
Governance	Secondary stakeholder	What are the proper governance and decision-making mechanisms to include secondary stakeholders during all the phases of a megaproject (not only in terms of project performance and success)?
	Reporting and disclosing strategy	What are the proper strategies, and approaches, to disclose and publicly report the impacts (predicted or assessed) of megaprojects?
	Dynamic and decentralized governance	What are the characteristics of a multi-dimensional and multi-purpose dynamic and decentralized governance for megaprojects?
Decision-making	Certifications	What is the relationship between scores obtained by megaprojects within the Envision rating system and the actual generated impacts during construction?
	Accounting strategies	What are the proper accounting approaches and methodologies to take into account local vs national, short- vs medium and long-term stakeholders' interests and generated Impacts?
Social and economic effect	Social/environmental vs economic impacts	What is the proper approach to evaluate, account and report social and environmental impacts in economic terms?
	Megaproject social responsibility framework	How can the generated impacts (social, economic and environmental) be included in a holistic decision-making framework?
	End of Life impacts	What are the impacts of the End of Life phase?
Risk Assessment	Disentangle complexity through causal relationships	What are the causal relationships among different impacts (social, economic and environmental) and stakeholders' actions in order to improve risk assessment?

Source: authors' own elaboration.

4.5. Summary

In this systematic literature review we addressed, with a broad and holistic point of view, the role that accounting studies played and are playing for megaprojects and sustainable infrastructure. 254 scientific contributions have been firstly analyzed through meta-analysis and quantitative evaluation of top contributing authors, countries and journals to provide a first overview about the analyzed corpus of literature. Findings revealed how the literature related to megaprojects and economic, social or environmental aspects started an exponential growth only since 2010, and the scientific contributions are mainly derived from a few international journals (international journal of project management, international journal of managing projects in business, and engineering, construction and architectural management), thus still remaining far from accounting studies. This first result shows how past literature has been dominated by a technical and managerial vision (project management) of megaprojects and the contribution of accounting is still very limited. The most central author (and corresponding work) is undoubtedly Flyvbjerg (2014). The top contributing countries are the US, UK, China and Australia. Finally, from the co-occurrence keywords network, five main branches emerged: project management, governance, decision-making, social and economic effects, and risk assessment.

Consequently, the five topics have been analyzed in detail by classifying them with respect to the project phases (front-end, construction, use, end of life), the considered impacts (environmental, social, economic) and the aim and type of analysis based on the six stages of SROI analysis: from stage 1 (identifying stakeholders) to stage 6 (reporting, using and embedding). Findings revealed how the majority of research works still focus on project management and on the technical side, although in recent years a more holistic vision about impacts is emerging. In addition, there is a lack of studies about use and especially post-use/end of life phases. Similarly, most of the literature addressed the first stages of SROI analysis – identifying stakeholders, mapping outcomes, establishing impacts. Only a few studies attempted to translate social or environmental impacts in economic and financial terms (stage 3 and 5). Moreover, the understanding of the relationships between reporting activities (stage 6) and project performance and success is understudied. Finally, novel methodologies and models have still to be fully developed and understood. For instance, decentralized megaprojects (instead of traditional centralized ones) in urban settings or for tourism development are still at their infancy. Similarly, untangling the complexity of megaprojects in a causal fashion through methodologies such as system dynamics and thinking, focusing on relationships among actors, various management factors, and generated impacts currently is almost completely absent from the literature.

Concluding, this literature review revealed several research gaps and future directions for research: accounting impacts during the use, post-use, and end of life phases, analyzing the influence and different strategies for reporting activities, translating, or comparing, generated impacts in economic and financial terms, untangling causalities in megaprojects complex systems. In general, what emerged is that the role of accounting for the megaproject development is all still to be played out.

References

Adityanandana, M. & Gerber, J.F. (2019). Post-growth in the Tropics? Contestations over Tri Hita Karana and a tourism megaproject in Bali. *Journal of Sustainable Tourism*, 27(12), 1839–1856.

Agarchand, N. & Laishram, B. (2017). Sustainable infrastructure development challenges through PPP procurement process: Indian perspective. *International Journal of Managing Projects in Business*, 10(3), 642–662.

Aria, M. & Cuccurullo, C. (2017). Bibliometrix: An R-tool for comprehensive science mapping analysis. *Journal of Informetrics*, 11(4), 959–975.

Badi, S., Rocher, W. & Ochieng, E. (2020). The impact of social power and influence on the implementation of innovation strategies: A case study of a UK mega infrastructure construction project. *European Management Journal*, 38(5), 736–749.

Barrett, M. (1979). Environmental impact statements. *Omega*, 7(5), 431–439.

Bowerman, G. (2021). *Industry Perspective: Vietnam Confronts Dual Forces in Tourism Development: Sustainable Initiatives Versus Megaproject Investments*, 18(6). http://ertr.tamu.eduhttp//ertr.tamu.edu.

Brunet, M. & Aubry, M. (2018). The governance of major public infrastructure projects: the process of translation. *International Journal of Managing Projects in Business*, 11(1), 80–103.

Caldas, C. & Gupta, A. (2017). Critical factors impacting the performance of mega-projects. *Engineering, Construction and Architectural Management*, 24(6), 920–934.

Camargo, B.A. & Vázquez-Maguirre, M. (2021). Humanism, dignity and indigenous justice: the mayan train megaproject, Mexico. *Journal of Sustainable Tourism*, 29(2–3), 371–390.

Cepeda, D.M., Sohail, M. & Ogunlowo, O.O. (2018). Understanding the critical success factors for delivery of megaprojects in Colombia. *Proceedings of Institution of Civil Engineers: Management, Procurement and Law*, *171*(2), 45–57.

Cerić, A., Vukomanović, M., Ivić, I. & Kolarić, S. (2021). Trust in megaprojects: A comprehensive literature review of research trends. *International Journal of Project Management*, *39*(4), 325–338.

Chang, C.Y. (2013). Understanding the hold-up problem in the management of megaprojects: The case of the Channel Tunnel Rail Link project. *International Journal of Project Management*, *31*(4), 628–637.

Chen, X., He, Q., Zhang, X., Cao, T. & Liu, Y. (2021). What motivates stakeholders to engage in collaborative innovation in the infrastructure megaprojects? *Journal of Civil Engineering and Management*, *27*(8), 579–594.

Chi, M., Chong, H.Y. & Xu, Y. (2022). The effects of shared vision on value co-creation in megaprojects: A multigroup analysis between clients and main contractors. *International Journal of Project Management*, *40*(3), 218–234.

Connor-Lajambe, H. (1990). Societal impacts of utility overinvestment. The James Bay hydroelectric project. *Utilities Policy*, 78–87.

Cristiano, S. & Gonella, F. (2019). To build or not to build? Megaprojects, resources, and environment: An emergy synthesis for a systemic evaluation of a major highway expansion. *Journal of Cleaner Production*, *223*, 772–789.

Dal Mas, F., Massaro, M., Lombardi, R. & Garlatti, A. (2019). From output to outcome measures in the public sector: a structured literature review. *International Journal of Organizational Analysis*.

Daye, M., Charman, K., Wang, Y. & Suzhikova, B. (2020). Exploring local stakeholders' views on the prospects of China's Belt & Road Initiative on tourism development in Kazakhstan. *Current Issues in Tourism*, *23*(15), 1948–1962.

De Meo, P., Ferrara, E., Fiumara, G. & Provetti, A. (2011). Generalized louvain method for community detection in large networks. In *2011 11th International Conference on Intelligent Systems Design and Applications*, Cordoba, Spain, 88–93.

Derakhshan, R., Turner, R. & Mancini, M. (2019). Project governance and stakeholders: a literature review. *International Journal of Project Management*, *37*(1), 98–116.

Destyanto, A.R., Hidayatno, A. & Amalia, A. (2017). Analysis of the effects of Co2 emissions from coal-fired power plants on the gross domestic regional product in Jakarta. *International Journal of Technology*, *8*(7), 1345–1355.

Di Maddaloni, F. & Davis, K. (2017). The influence of local community stakeholders in megaprojects: Rethinking their inclusiveness to improve project performance. *International Journal of Project Management*, 35(8), 1537–1556.

Dogan, E. & Stupar, A. (2017). The limits of growth: A case study of three mega-projects in Istanbul. *Cities*, 60, 281–288.

Dumay, J., Bernardi, C., Guthrie, J. & Demartini, P. (2016). Integrated reporting: A structured literature review. *Accounting Forum*, 40(3), 166–185.

Dyer, R. (2017). Cultural sense-making integration into risk mitigation strategies towards megaproject success. *International Journal of Project Management*, 35(7), 1338–1349.

Erie, S.P. & MacKenzie, S.A. (2010). Southern California's crown jewels: Historical governance and finance lessons. *Public Works Management and Policy*, 14(3), 205–245.

Fahri, J., Biesenthal, C., Pollack, J. & Sankaran, S. (2015). Understanding megaproject success beyond the project close-out stage. *Construction Economics and Building*, 15(3), 48–58.

Flyvbjerg, B. (2014). What you should know about megaprojects and why: An overview. *Project Management Journal*, 45(2), 6–19.

Flyvbjerg, B., Bruzelius, N. & Rothengatter, W. (2003). Megaprojects and Risk. In *Megaprojects and Risk*. Cambridge University Press.

Forliano, C., De Bernardi, P. & Yahiaoui, D. (2021). Entrepreneurial universities: A bibliometric analysis within the business and management domains. *Technological Forecasting and Social Change*, 165, 120522.

German Cooperation and UNEP. (2022). *Sustainable Infrastructure Tool Navigator*. https://sustainable-infrastructure-tools.org/.

Giezen, M. (2012). Keeping it simple? A case study into the advantages and disadvantages of reducing complexity in mega project planning. *International Journal of Project Management*, 30(7), 781–790.

Golubchikov, O. (2017). From a sports mega-event to a regional megaproject: the Sochi winter Olympics and the return of geography in state development priorities. *International Journal of Sport Policy*, 9(2), 237–255.

Gosasang, V., Yip, T.L. & Chandraprakaikul, W. (2018). Long-term container throughput forecast and equipment planning: the case of Bangkok Port. *Maritime Business Review*, 3(1), 53–69.

Griffiths, F. (1989). Project contract strategy for 1992 and beyond. *International Journal of Project Management*, 7(2), 69–83.

Hamman, E. (2016). The influence of environmental NGOs on project finance: a case study of activism, development and Australia's Great Barrier Reef. *Journal of Sustainable Finance and Investment*, 6(1), 51–66.

Hidayatno, A., Moeis, A.O., Sutrisno, A. & Maulidiah, W. (2015). Risk impact analysis on the investment of drinking water supply system development using project risk management. *International Journal of Technology*, 6(5), 894–904.

Horwitch, M. (1990). From unitary to distributed objectives. The changing nature of major projects. *Technology in Society*, 12(2), 173–195.

Hu, Y., Chan, A.P.C., Le, Y., Jiang, W.-P., Xie, L.-L. & Hon, C.H.K. (2012). Improving Megasite Management Performance through Incentives: Lessons Learned from the Shanghai Expo Construction. *Journal of Management in Engineering*, 28(3), 330–337.

Inter-American Development Bank (2018). *What is Sustainable Infrastructure? A Framework to Guide Sustainability Across the Project Cycle*.

Invernizzi, D.C., Locatelli, G., Grönqvist, M. & Brookes, N.J. (2019). Applying value management when it seems that there is no value to be managed: the case of nuclear decommissioning. *International Journal of Project Management*, 37(5), 668–683.

Jain, M. & Rohracher, H. (2022). Assessing transformative change of infrastructures in urban area redevelopments. *Cities*, 124.

Jia, G., Yang, F., Wang, G., Hong, B. & You, R. (2011). A study of mega project from a perspective of social conflict theory. *International Journal of Project Management*, 29(7), 817–827.

Kanwal, S., Rasheed, M.I., Pitafi, A.H., Pitafi, A. & Ren, M. (2020). Road and transport infrastructure development and community support for tourism: The role of perceived benefits, and community satisfaction. *Tourism Management*, 77.

Kardes, I., Ozturk, A., Cavusgil, S.T. & Cavusgil, E. (2013). Managing global megaprojects: Complexity and risk management. *International Business Review*, 22(6), 905–917.

Kim, S.G. (2010). Risk performance indexes and measurement systems for mega construction projects. *Journal of Civil Engineering and Management*, 16(4), 586–594.

Kumaraswamy, M.M., Ling, F.Y.Y., Anvuur, A.M. & Rahman, M.M. (2007). Targeting relationally integrated teams for sustainable PPPS. *Engineering, Construction and Architectural Management*, 14(6), 581–596.

Lee, C., Won, J.W., Jang, W., Jung, W., Han, S.H. & Kwak, Y.H. (2017). Social conflict management framework for project viability: Case studies from Korean megaprojects. *International Journal of Project Management*, 35(8), 1683–1696.

Leksin, V.N. & Porfiryev, B.N. (2015). Redevelopment of the arctic area of Russia as an objective of systems research and special-purpose program management methodological issues. *Economy of Region*, (4), 9–20.

Lenferink, S., Tillema, T. & Arts, J. (2013). Towards sustainable infrastructure development through integrated contracts: Experiences with inclusiveness in Dutch infrastructure projects. *International Journal of Project Management*, 31(4), 615–627.

Li, P., Liu, Z.-M., Fan, J. & Li, W.-H. (2018). Adaptive Control Theory and Index System for Social Stability Risk Assessment of Major Projects: Based on 22 Typical Cases. *International Journal of Information and Management Sciences*, 29, 381–402.

Li, Y., Han, Y., Luo, M. & Zhang, Y. (2019). *Impact of Megaproject Governance on Project Performance: Dynamic Governance of the Nanning Transportation Hub in China*.

Liberati, A., Altman, D.G., Tetzlaff, J., Mulrow, C., Gøtzsche, P.C., Ioannidis, J.P.A., Clarke, M., Devereaux, P.J., Kleijnen, J. & Moher, D. (2009). The PRISMA statement for reporting systematic reviews and meta-analyses of studies that evaluate health care interventions: explanation and elaboration. *Journal of Clinical Epidemiology*, 62(10), e1–e34.

Lin, H., Zeng, S., Ma, H., Zeng, R. & Tam, V.W.Y. (2017). An indicator system for evaluating megaproject social responsibility. *International Journal of Project Management*, 35(7), 1415–1426.

Litman, T. & Brenman, M. (2012). *A new social equity agenda for sustainable transportation*. Victoria Transport Policy Institute.

Little, R.G. (2011). The emerging role of public-private partnerships in megaproject delivery. *Public Works Management and Policy*, 16(3), 240–249.

Liu, J. & Ma, G. (2020). Study on incentive and supervision mechanisms of technological innovation in megaprojects based on the principal-agent theory. *Engineering, Construction and Architectural Management*, 28(6), 1593–1614.

Liu, Ze-zhao, Zhu, Zheng-wei, Wang, Hui-jia & Huang, J. (2016). Handling social risks in government-driven mega project: An empirical case study from West China. *International Journal of Project Management*, 34(2), 202–218.

Lopez del Puerto, C. & Shane, J.S. (2014). Keys to Success in Megaproject Management in Mexico and the United States: Case Study. *Journal of Construction Engineering and Management*, 140(4).

Ma, H., Liu, Z., Zeng, S., Lin, H. & Tam, V.W.Y. (2020). Does megaproject social responsibility improve the sustainability of the construction industry? *Engineering, Construction and Architectural Management*, 27(4), 975–996.

Ma, H., Liu, Z., Zeng, S., Lin, H. & Tam, V.W.Y. (2020). Does megaproject social responsibility improve the sustainability of the construction industry? *Engineering, Construction and Architectural Management*, 27(4), 975–996.

Ma, L. & Fu, H. (2022). A Governance Framework for the Sustainable Delivery of Megaprojects: The Interaction of Megaproject Citizenship Behavior and Contracts. *Journal of Construction Engineering and Management*, 148(4).

Mainga, W. (2017). Examining project learning, project management competencies, and project efficiency in project-based firms (PBFs). *International Journal of Managing Projects in Business*, 10(3), 454–504.

Maldonado, M.O. & Corbey, M. (2016). Social return on investment (SROI): a review of the technique. *Maandblad Voor Account. Bedrifsecon*, 90, 79–87.

Massaro, M., Dumay, J. & Guthrie, J. (2016). On the shoulders of giants: undertaking a structured literature review in accounting. *Accounting, Auditing and Accountability Journal*, 29(5), 767–801.

McCoy, H.A. & Singer, J.F. (1978). Research notes on socioeconomic siting dynamics. *Socio-Economic Planning Sciences*, 12(3), 153–159.

McWhirter, N. & Shealy, T. (2018). Pedagogy and Evaluation of an Envision Case Study Module Bridging Sustainable Engineering and Behavioral Science. *Journal of Professional Issues in Engineering Education and Practice*, 144(4).

Moher, D., Liberati, A., Tetzlaff, J. & Altman, D.G. (2010). Preferred reporting items for systematic reviews and meta-analyses: The PRISMA statement. *International Journal of Surgery*, 8(5), 336–341.

Morris, P.W.G. & Geraldi, J. (2011). Managing the institutional context for projects. *Project Management Journal*, 42(6), 20–32.

Mostafa, M.A. & El-Gohary, N.M. (2015). Semantic System for Stakeholder-Conscious Infrastructure Project Planning and Design. *Journal of Construction Engineering and Management*, 141(2), 04014075.

Mulholland, C., Chan, P.W., Canning, K. & Ejohwomu, O.A. (2020). Social value for whom, by whom and when? Managing stakeholder dynamics in a UK megaproject. *Proceedings of Institution of Civil Engineers: Management, Procurement and Law*, 173(2), 75–86.

Nicholls, J., Lawlor, E., Neitzert, E., Goodspeed, T., Cupitt, S., Durie, S., Inglis, J., Leathem, K., Lumley, T. & Piper, R. (2012). *A guide to Social Return on Investment*. https://socialvalueuk.org/wp-content/uploads/2016/03/The Guide to Social Return on Investment 2015.pdf.

Nourelfath, M., Lababidi, H.M.S. & Aldowaisan, T. (2022). Socioeconomic impacts of strategic oil and gas megaprojects: A case study in Kuwait. *International Journal of Production Economics*, 246.

Nyarirangwe, M. & Babatunde, O.K. (2019). Megaproject complexity attributes and competences: lessons from IT and construction projects. *International Journal of Information Systems and Project Management*, 7(4), 77–99.

OECD. (2019). *Sustainable Infrastructure for Low-Carbon Development in Central Asia and the Caucasus*.

Paul, J. & Criado, A.R. (2020). The art of writing literature review: What do we know and what do we need to know? *International Business Review*, 29(4).

Priemus, H. (2010). Mega-projects: Dealing with Pitfalls. *European Planning Studies*, 18(7), 1023–1039.

Project Management Institute. (2017). *A guide to the project management body of knowledge (PMBOK guide)*. 6th ed. Project Management Institute.

Qiu, Y., Chen, H., Sheng, Z. & Cheng, S. (2019). Governance of institutional complexity in megaproject organizations. *International Journal of Project Management*, 37(3), 425–443.

Randeree, K. (2014). Reputation and Mega-project Management: Lessons from Host Cities of the Olympic Games. In *Change Management: An International Journal*, 13(2). http://ijmc.cgpublisher.com/product/pub.253/prod.30.

Rehman, O.U., Liu, X., Rauf, A., Slama, M., Ben & Amin, W. (2020). Internet tradition and tourism development: A causality analysis on BRI listed economies. *Tourism Economics*, 26(6), 926–957.

Rocha, G. de M. & Neves, M.B. (2018). Hydroelectric projects and territorial Governance in regions of the state of Pará, Brazilian Amazon. *Entrepreneurship and Sustainability Issues*, 5(4), 712–723.

Roelich, K., Knoeri, C., Steinberger, J.K., Varga, L., Blythe, P.T., Butler, D., Gupta, R., Harrison, G.P., Martin, C. & Purnell, P. (2015). Towards resource-efficient and service-oriented integrated infrastructure operation. *Technological Forecasting and Social Change*, 92, 40–52.

Sabin, P.R. (1995). Impact of channel tunnel. *Journal of Professional Issues in Engineering Education and Practice*, 121(4), 231–232.

Sandhu, M. & Khan, A. (2017). Benchmarking project management dimensions at the lapse of a century: Case of Panama Canal and Palm Diera Island mega projects. *Benchmarking*, 24(6), 1675–1689.

Särkilahti, M., Kinnunen, V., Kettunen, R., Jokinen, A. & Rintala, J. (2017). Replacing centralised waste and sanitation infrastructure with local treatment and nutrient recycling: Expert opinions in the context of urban planning. *Technological Forecasting and Social Change*, 118, 195–204.

Shakirova, S. (2015). Country images of Kazakhstan: From stereotypes and critique to positive national branding. *Journal of Eastern European and Central Asian Research*, 2(1).

Shealy, T. & Klotz, L. (2015). Well-Endowed Rating Systems: How Modified Defaults Can Lead to More Sustainable Performance. *Journal of Construction Engineering and Management*, 141(10).

Shealy, T., Klotz, L., Weber, E.U., Johnson, E.J. & Bell, R.G. (2016). Using Framing Effects to Inform More Sustainable Infrastructure Design Decisions. *Journal of Construction Engineering and Management*, 142(9), 04016037.

Sroka, R. (2021). Mega-projects and mega-events: evaluating Vancouver 2010 stadium and convention infrastructure. *Journal of Sport and Tourism*, 25(3), 183–200.

Stone, R. (2008). Three Gorges Dam: Into the Unknown. *Science*, 321(5889), 628–632.

Sykes, A. (1990). Macro Projects Status, Prospects, and the Need for International Cooperation. *Technology in Society*, 12, 157–172.

Teo, M.M.M. & Loosemore, M. (2010). Community-based protest against construction projects: The social determinants of protest movement continuity. *International Journal of Managing Projects in Business*, 3(2), 216–235.

Thacker, S., Adshead, D., Fay, M., Hallegatte, S., Harvey, M., Meller, H., O'Regan, N., Rozenberg, J., Watkins, G. & Hall, J.W. (2019). Infrastructure for sustainable development. *Nature Sustainability*, 2(4), 324–331.

Turner, J.R. & Xue, Y. (2018). On the success of megaprojects. *International Journal of Managing Projects in Business*, 11(3), 783–805.

United Nations (2001). *Indicators Of Sustainable Development: Framework And Methodologies, Background Paper No. 3*.

van Dijk, T. (2021). Strategic spatial planning through pragmatic blueprints: Forms and levels of adaptivity in modernist planning of the Dutch IJsselmeerpolders. *Futures*, 125.

van Marrewijk, A., Ybema, S., Smits, K., Clegg, S. & Pitsis, T. (2016). Clash of the Titans: Temporal Organizing and Collaborative Dynamics in the Panama Canal Megaproject. *Organization Studies*, 37(12), 1745–1769.

von Branconi, C. & Loch, C.H. (2004). Contracting for major projects: Eight business levers for top management. *International Journal of Project Management*, 22(2), 119–130.

Wang, D., Fu, H. & Fang, S. (2020). The efficacy of trust for the governance of uncertainty and opportunism in megaprojects: The moderating role of contractual control. *Engineering, Construction and Architectural Management*, 27(1), 150–167.

Wei, H.-H., Liu, M., Skibniewski, M.J. & Balali, V. (2016). Prioritizing Sustainable Transport Projects through Multicriteria Group Decision Making: Case Study of Tianjin Binhai New Area, China. *Journal of Management in Engineering*, 32(5), 04016010.

Wessels, M. (2014). Stimulating sustainable infrastructure development through public-private partnerships. *Proceedings of Institution of Civil Engineers: Management, Procurement and Law*, 167(5), 232–241.

Whitty, S.J. & Maylor, H. (2009). And then came Complex Project Management (revised). *International Journal of Project Management*, 27(3), 304–310.

Zeng, R., Chini, A. & Ries, R. (2021). Innovative design for sustainability: Integrating embodied impacts and costs during the early design phase. *Engineering, Construction and Architectural Management*, 28(3), 747–764.

Zheng, L. (2020). Research on the impact of mega-projects on carrying capacity of cities taking the first-line project of the West-East gas pipeline as an example. *Journal of Management Science and Engineering*, 5(3), 195–211.

Zhou, Z. & Mi, C. (2017). Social responsibility research within the context of megaproject management: Trends, gaps and opportunities. *International Journal of Project Management*, 35(7), 1378–1390.

Zidane, Y.J.-T., Hussein, B.A., Johansen, A. & Andersen, B. (2016). PESTOL-framework for «project evaluation on strategic, tactical and operational levels». *International Journal of Information Systems and Project Management*, 4(3), 25–41.

Chapter 5
ENVIRONMENTAL JUSTICE MOVEMENT: SOCIAL AND ENVIRONMENTAL CONFLICTS

ABSTRACT: *This chapter discusses the rise and emergence of the global environmental justice movement and its relationship with infrastructure systems and megaprojects. First, a brief introduction to the main topics and definitions related to environmental justice, with a historical overview, is provided, and, second, several case studies reported by the Environmental Justice Atlas (EJAtlas) and by scientific and gray literature are reported and discussed. Finally, the impact of social and environmental conflicts on megaprojects and infrastructure performance is discussed by giving some insights for a more holistic and systemic vision for megaprojects' management in order to consider causalities among the three pillars of sustainability.*

SUMMARY: 5.1. The emergence of the environmental justice movement. – 5.1.1. About free riders, commons and distributional economics. – 5.2. Conflicts and megaprojects: the challenge of stakeholders' management. – 5.3. Toward an inclusive and systemic management of infrastructure projects. – 5.4. Summary. – References.

5.1. The emergence of the environmental justice movement

Since the second post-war and the subsequent period of economic recovery in the 1950s and 1960s the economic models clashed and entered into conflicts with the management, the preservation and conservation of the natural environment and the local and global resources. This clash can be simply described in terms of the social metabolism and extractive practices of our society that first appropriates, then transforms and finally disposes materials and energy to and from the environment (Fischer-Kowalski & Haberl, 1997, 2015; Martinez-Alier, Temper & Demaria, 2016; Padovan, 2000).

Quoting Martinez-Alier, Temper, Del Bene, et al. (2016, p. 1) "*energy cannot be recycled [....] materials are recycled only in part, and therefore even an economy that did not grow would need fresh supplies*". Indeed, our economy, as well as the physical world, "*is not circular, it is entropic*" (Haas et al., 2015). In this sense, since the resources, materials or energy provided by the environment are not infinite, a *just* management and distribution is crucial to guarantee fair rights and equity for everyone. Ecological distribution (Joan, 1995), thus, becomes crucial to avoid the rising of inequalities, injustices for every human or non-human entity and to prevent the emergence of ecological conflicts. The problem of distribution of resources is not novel, and has been studied since the Second World War by Garrett Hardin, Carol Rose, and Elinor Ostrom (and other thinkers and schools of thought), who respectively introduced the Commons and the free rider dilemma, discussed the multiplicative properties of non-tangible Commons, such as the culture and the arts, and proposed the solution to the free rider dilemma by defining eight simple rules for the management of the Commons.

In this chapter, we first discuss the emergence of the debate related to the Commons, the distributional problems and their managerial solutions, and, second, we discuss the rise of the global environmental justice movement at a global scale. The origin and the evolution of the environmental justice movement, then, is introduced by providing examples of social and environmental conflicts, related to infrastructure projects, as reported and classified by the Environmental Justice Atlas (EJAtlas). Finally, the relation and connection between conflicts and megaprojects and infrastructure's performance is briefly discussed by highlighting the complex causalities among environmental issues, the rise of protests and environmental and social conflicts and their impacts on the planning, construction and use of large infrastructures.

5.1.1. About free riders, commons and distributional economics

The debate about resource and value distribution has a long history. It is strictly connected to the theory of value and may be traced back to the historical *enclosure act* in the United Kingdom, which provoked earlier forms of social protests related to value and resource distribution (Rifkin, 2014). From these very first declared appropriation acts onwards, for more than two hundred years the value creation has been strictly coupled to the appropriation and extraction of resources (raw materials, energy, lands, air quality, ...) aiming at capital accumulation by a bunch (i.e., the minority of the society) of capitalists and owners (Mazzucato, 2018). In parallel, since then the economic and value theory followed the mainstream schools of thought (although critics were already in place in the XIX century) of eternal economic growth, without caring about boundaries, limits or equal and just value distribution.

The academic debate regarding distribution, and the protection and management of *limited* natural resources – and the emergence of a solution (*a problem well stated is half solved*) – officially emerged more than two hundred years after the first British enclosure, and more than one hundred years after the formulation of the earlier economic and value national theories. With the groundbreaking work of Garrett Hardin, the "*Tragedy of the Commons*", the focus was not yet directly related to environmental justice and/or a distributional theory, but rather on highlighting the need of "*a fundamental extension in morality*" to solve the Malthusian issue of the lack of resources, i.e., the exponential population growth problem versus the linear growth of food production, because, quoting again Hardin, "*a finite world can support only a finite population*" (G. Hardin, 1968, 1998). In particular, Hardin in his seminal paper, introduced the concept of the *free rider* – i.e., *someone who receives a benefit without contributing toward the cost of its production* (R. Hardin & Cullity, 2003) – and the unfair appropriation of finite common resources. Although the hypothesis and premises were partially wrong and still based on the Malthusian view (i.e., the population grows exponentially indefinitely with a proper amount of resources), the work of Hardin firstly highlighted the need to discuss resource appropriation and distribution. A few decades later, the environmental debate fully entered into the academic community, as well as in the public debate, with the birth of environmental economic theories and earlier environmental thinkers, such as Herman Daly or Kenneth Boulding. The solution to the free riders dilemma and the management of the Commons was then treated in the 1980s in two different ways by, on one side, Carol Rose, who introduced "*the Comedy of the Commons*", and, on the other side, Elinor Ostrom with her study on "*Governing the Commons*", who faced with the management of the so-called common pool resources (CPR). Carol Rose discussed intangible and immaterial resources, such as culture, for which a reinforcing loop and a different rule exists – i.e., *the more the merrier* – rather than a limited amount to be managed, such as in the case of raw materials or lands. In this case, indeed, the distributional problem is simply reduced to an accessibility problem to such resources and not to the free rider dilemma or to extreme or unbalanced appropriation (Rose, 1986). On the other side, Elinor Ostrom, who won the Nobel Memorial Prize in Economic Sciences for her work on the management of the Commons, identified a few (eight) principles to manage a long-enduring CPR, allowing its long-term usage without exploiting it for the benefit of a minority (for a free rider and/or a capitalist accumulation). Among other principles, Elinor Ostrom introduced the idea to have specific roles in the communities who need to manage a CPR such as the *monitors,* who need to control the *appropriators*, and eventually apply *graduated sanctions*, and to have specific and *clearly defined boundaries* (who is affected/involved), *collective-choice arrangements*, and *conflict-resolution mechanism* (Ostrom, 1990).

However, despite the great effort to model and introduce environmental constraints into the economic theories and/or to understand how to manage resources in a safe and just way, from the 1960s, the parallel issues of environmental justice and the distributional issue started to be crucial to understand and decode the increasing (in number and in intensity) social conflicts. During the 1970s and the 1980s, various conflicts were indeed generated by unfair and unjust allocation of environmental resources, giving birth to the *ecological distribution conflicts*. In this sense, according to Temper et al. (2018) an ecological distribution conflict is *"a collective action (such as writing of petitions, demonstrations, blockades, etc...), induced by existing or anticipated environmental pollution or damage to nature affecting communities, which has been caused or will be caused by increases or changes in the social metabolism"*. In other words, an ecological distribution conflict, similar to what occurred in the last two centuries of capitalism for economic distribution struggles and class conflicts, is provoked by an unfair environmental distribution. Ecological distribution conflicts, thus, are strictly connected and linked to the concept of *environmental justice* (Martinez-Alier & O'Connor, 1995). As reported and discussed by Bullard (1996) the *Environmental Justice Movement* derived from the *environmental racism* conducted in the United States of America during all the 1970s and 1980s. *"Persistent injustice toward 'people of color' in the United States"* have been widely reported in the past decades (Martinez-Alier et al., 2016, p. 2) such as the segregation of Latin or black people to most polluted neighbourhoods, to areas close to landfills and/or incinerators, or with the lack of basic health, aesthetic and natural services. Such practices were related to income-level (a *class* and economic problem) but not exclusively. Environmental racist practices, indeed, were widely perpetrated by applying such ecological discrimination simply based on race, gender, or religion (Bullard, 1996) by giving rise to wide and participated social movements during the 1980s in the major United States cities. Similar ecological unfair distributions have been recently reported in terms of climate change impact and for the most affected classes or people (Ellena et al., 2020; Melis et al., 2023). For instance, Ellena et al. (2023) studied social inequalities in the city of Turin in Italy by highlighting the different impacts (number of deaths caused by extreme hot temperatures) of urban heat island (as effect of climate change) on people with different age, education, marital status, as well as on people living in different areas with differences on environmental and outdoor factors, such as the presence of natural parks, trees, or service facilities. As a symbol of social inequalities, again in the city of Turin, the average life expectancy has been analyzed along a public transportation line by discovering a loss of 5 months of life expectancy every kilometre (Stagliano, 2016). Basically, such unfair environmental distribution led to the emergence of an *"intersectional socio-environmental movement"* (Menton et al., 2020). As a consequence, in 1991, after more than a decade of environmental conflicts and injustices, the *Principles of Environmental*

Justice were published at the "*First National People of Colour Environmental Leadership Summit*" in Washington, DC. The 17 principles focused, among other aspects, on the affirmation of Mother Earth's sacredness and the right to be free from ecological destruction, the affirmation of peoples' rights to self-determination, demands for participation rights, as well as the rejection of military occupation, repression, and exploitation of lands, peoples, cultures, and other life forms (Menton et al., 2020).

What the emergence of the environmental justice movement demonstrated was that the concept of environmental justice is much more complex than simply being a resource distribution problem. The concept of justice, indeed, includes, first, a distributional issue – which only appears in case of scarcity and not in the case of the comedy of the commons (Rose, 1986) – and rules on how to reduce inequalities (Wenz, 1996), but also on how to manage intergenerational justice (Rawls, 1996). These distinctions and competition between short-term and long-term impacts, between local and international value distribution and between public and private interests become even clearer and more relevant when considering large infrastructures or mega-projects. As discussed in chapters 2 and 3 on sustainable and critical infrastructure, to understand such distinctions, one can think about, for instance, a large transportation infrastructure such as a new airport, like the widely contested megaproject for the new Notre-Dame-des-Landes airport in the North of France (Algostino, 2016; Burballa-Noria, 2018; Florez et al., 2022). In that megaproject, the long-term national economic interests competed with short and medium-term local communities' land rights, citizens' long-term and global environmental interests against a new polluting transportation hub, in opposition with short-term and local (regional or national) political and economic interests, and so on. Similarly, the European strategy and long-term plan for the Trans European Transport Network (TEN-T) – regulated by the European Directive 1315/2013 [1] (The European Parliament and the Council, 2013) – in the past decade encountered strong opposition from local communities and social movements. Hence, understanding the roots and foundations of the environmental justice movement and the unjust and unfair ecological or value distributions becomes crucial to fully grasp the underlying causes of social protests against megaprojects (Florez et al., 2022).

In this sense, according to Menton et al. (2020), the mainstream Environmental Justice framework relies on four different dimensions of justice,

---

[1] Regulation (EU) No 1315/2013 of the European Parliament and of the Council of 11 December 2013 on Union guidelines for the development of the trans-European transport network and repealing Decision No. 661/2010/EU.

including the 1) distributional, 2) recognitional, 3) procedural and 4) capabilities approach. The former two (i.e., distributional and recognitional) focused on equal distribution of ecological costs and benefits in terms of both environmental services (materials, resources, energy) and social (wealth, access to social services, ...) and on the "*recognition*" of equal opportunity and "*personal dignity of all individuals*" (p. 1624), while the latter two refer to the institutional (procedural justice) and individual (capabilities) procedures. In particular, the capabilities approach focuses not only on the mere distribution of resources, but on the opportunities that such resources may generate. In this sense, in terms of megaprojects, the four different environmental justice views become fundamental for a variety of reasons, starting from lands' right of local communities (distributional justice), to the preservation of local identities, culture and economies (recognitional), up to the democratic debate and top-down imposition that often occurs (Florez et al., 2022) (procedural justice) or the unfair long-term distribution of outcomes and impacts.[2] Indeed, social protests against megaprojects are typically provoked by an unfair distribution of impacts (not outputs), since typically local communities should sacrifice their wellbeing for long-term and wider (in terms of space) 'positive' impacts. In this sense, megaprojects typically act in an extractive fashion (largely discussed in the social metabolism literature on urban environment) by, first, extracting and adding value from natural local resources such as public lands, forests, commons and, then, moving and distributing it to the private sector (firms but also private citizens) not belonging to the exploited territory.

Although all attempts to define a global environmental justice movement, both from the activist or the academic side, the environmental justice concept is not uniquely defined. There are many similar, and in certain cases interchangeable terms used worldwide in the past decades. Whereas in the United States the Environmental Justice was the most adopted term, in India and Latin America many academics referred to a similar concept by defining the "*environmentalism of the poor*" (Martinez-Alier, 2003; Nixon, 2011). More recently, the term climate justice has become widespread to refer, on one side, to extractive practices specifically of fossil fuels or to any human activities with impact on climate change and carbon dioxide emissions and, on the other side, to initiative to promote local public sustainable transportation systems or any initiative to reduce greenhouse gas emis-

---

[2] Roughly speaking, outcomes differentiate from output in terms of timespan (short vs long-term impacts) and in terms of physical vs intangible impacts (on wellbeing for instance). For a specific and detailed discussion about outputs, outcomes and impacts of megaprojects see for instance Zidane et al. (2016).

sions (Martinez-Alier et al., 2016). From the theoretical and academic debate (see previous paragraph on the Commons), in the 1980s the Commons movements emerged and gained wide visibility thanks also to the effort of computer scientists and activists which began a 'war' to defend physical and intangible commons (Rifkin, 2014). Grounded on the precursory studies of Hardin, Rose and Ostrom, the Commons became central in the 1980s thanks to the introduction of the first copyleft software licenses (see for instance the GNU GPL) with which activists all around the world openly declared the war to the large IT firms and corporations. In parallel, the environmental and social protests emerged to defend local Commons (rivers, forests, lands, water sources).

Concluding this brief excursus about the environmental justice movement, alongside the mainstream environmental justice framework, recently, there are a few theoretical frameworks that are attempting to expand the boundaries of justice such as the *Critical Environmental Justice* (CEJ), *Ecological Justice* and *Intersectional Decolonial Environmental Justice* (IDEJ) (Menton et al., 2020). Briefly, CEJ attempts to expand the EJ boundaries to a less institutional point of view, Ecological Justice criticized the anthropocentric vision of environmental justice and expand the boundaries of justice to non-human entities, while IDEJ tries to consider the multi-faceted roots of injustice without reducing it to a single mono-dimension (e.g., economic, environmental, gender, race, …). Although a deep and detailed discussion is out of the scope of this chapter, in the next sections a few of the introduced aspects will be discussed by presenting some case studies, in order to show how a broad vision on environmental justice, and its further and most recent expansions, is necessary to an inclusive stakeholder management approach in megaprojects.

5.2. Conflicts and megaprojects: the challenge of stakeholders' management

In past decades, social and environmental conflicts rose worldwide against extractive and exploitative practices and in defence of Commons and natural limited resources. In this sense, Social Movement Theory (SMT) focuses on the underlying reasons, the modes and the outcomes of social protests and mobilizations (a more specific but different lens with respect to the environmental justice frameworks) (Martinez-Alier et al., 2016; Tarrow, 2005). Academics and activists constantly struggled to identify and study the best strategy according to the context (e.g., a new construction of an infrastructure or toxic discharge). Obviously, there are several different actions and types of ecological distribution conflicts, spanning from blockades, tree plantation resistances, coalitions building, financial divestments, and counter-accounting actions. Which action fits better depends on numerous factors, and there is not a *one-size-fits-all* solution. Nowadays, the largest database in the world regarding environmental justice and ecological distribution conflicts is represented by the Environmental Justice Atlas (EJAtlas), project led by the Institut de Ciència i Tecnologia Ambientals (ICTA) of the Universitat Autonoma de Barcelona (UAB) during the past decade (Martinez-Alier et al., 2016; Temper et al., 2015, 2018). The EJAtlas mapped and classified thousands of ecological distribution conflicts all around the world with a collaborative, iterative and participatory mapping process. Quoting its authors, the EJAtlas is a *"living document"*, from its conception and co-design to the ongoing collection and mapping process (Temper et al., 2015, p. 273).

According to the EJAtlas and their authors (Martinez-Alieret al., 2016) the most adopted actions are official complaint letters/petitions, public campaigns, street protests and marches, network building, involvement of international NGOs or media based activism. On the contrary, the less diffused practices correspond to boycotts of company products, refusal of compensations, threats to use arms, sabotage, financial activism or hunger strikes. From a quick sight, it is clear that the most common practices against environmental injustice follow soft practices to create consensus (more than 700 initiatives for each type have been identified by EJAtlas), while most radical actions such as sabotage or boycotts occur less frequently (dozens of times or less). Quite diffuse practices are counter-accounting initiatives (e.g., objections to the EIA) or community-based participatory research, too. Regarding the type of contested projects or infrastructure, a two level classification was adopted with 10 first-level macro-groups.[3] Among others, the majority of the contested projects were from rural areas (more than 60%) including mining (more than 1 out 5) and fossil fuels and industrial (almost 20%) projects, land grabbing (17%) and water management (14%) conflicts. The majority of the companies were fossil fuels companies (petrol, gas, ...) such as Royal Dutch Shell, Chevron Corporation, Exxon Mobil Corporation, mining or agro-industries corporations such as the Barrick Gold Corporation or the Monsanto Corporation (Martinez-Alier et al., 2016).

---

[3] Nuclear energy, mineral ores and buildings materials extraction, waste management, biomass and land conflicts, fossil fuels and climate justice/energy, infrastructure and built environment, water management, biodiversity conservation, industrial and utilities, tourism recreation.

Although in the Atlas thousands of different projects, from small to large or from infrastructure to illegal actions, are mapped and classified, the majority can be referred to large infrastructure projects. For instance, in Nigeria almost the totality of conflicts are against fossil fuel (petrol and gas) extraction plants, the construction of pipelines or accidents (such as explosions and petrol discharges in the sea). In Africa, in South America and in general in resource-rich developing countries, the majority of the conflicts refer to large extraction and mining infrastructure projects. On the contrary, in the European Union, the contested infrastructure are more diverse, including transportation infrastructure – high-speed railway lines (Esposito et al., 2021) or airports (Florez et al., 2022) – industrial facilities of petrol or gas companies, until tourism recreation facilities or water and waste discharge into the environment. For instance, in Tarragona (Spain) a petrochemical large complex, which provides almost 25% of total Spanish chemical production, provoked fatal health issues (cancer due to chemical exposure) and accidents (explosions in some plants) in the area of *la Canonja*. Several organizations denounced health and environmental risks in the past to the local administration that did not act and take any action against the complex, due to its economic impact on the territory. On the contrary, a very debated and contested megaproject was the illegal hotel in Algarrobico, Almeria, Spain. At the beginning of the century, an illegal hotel of 21-floors within the Cabo de Gata Nature reserve was (partially) built against national law on coastal natural environment protection and then, consequently, stopped. In the past twenty years, civil protests, petitions and other legal actions have been organized by citizens and national NGOs provoking a very complex public debate and a long legal trial – started in the earlier 2000s and ended in 2022 – against the company in charge of the construction (Azata Patrimonio SL). During the last 20 years, the construction was totally blocked with evident negative impacts, both on the company and on the landscape and the natural environment. Only in 2022, the construction was declared legal by the *Tribunal Superior de Justicia de Andalucía* (TSJA) by obliging to refund Azata for the economic losses suffered. Similarly and more recently, a megaproject again in the south of Spain provoked earlier social protests (currently, the megaproject is at the planning phase) starting from 2020 in Maro, near Malaga in Andalusia. Although in Europe many ecological distribution conflict examples may be found regarding any type of infrastructure, the most contested ones, in recent years, have been transportation megaprojects. The new planned airport near Paris – i.e., the Notre-Dame-des-Landes – represents one of the most significant wins obtained by the environmental justice movement. Indeed, the planned new airports provoked large and massive social protests that led to the land occupation (the land where the new airport should be built) and the creation of a ZAD (Zone À Defendre, in French) which obliged the government, on 17 January 2018, to withdraw the original plan and stop the project. A different output and result regards two Italian projects. The Trans Adriatic Pipeline (TAP) in Puglia in the South of Italy, i.e, an energy critical infrastructure project for a natural gas pipeline coming from the fields of Shah Deniz II in Azerbaijan to Italy, that has been widely contested by the local population and association, as well as by national and international NGOs but, the construction followed up. Similarly, the Turin-Lyon high-speed railway (HSR) line,[4] planned since the 1990s to connect Turin in Italy and Lyon in France by empowering the existing railway and tunnel across the Alps, has been widely and strongly contested for more than twenty years (as explained in Chapter 6). However, despite the mass protests and demonstrations, the project was officially started in 2020, after several Environmental Impact Assessment studies, public and political debates, changes of construction plans and many other legal, social and environmental issues.

5.3. Toward an inclusive and systemic management of infrastructure projects

Drawing on the environmental justice principles and debate, it is now clear that infrastructural territorialization projects, as discussed in chapters 1-3, and megaprojects or infrastructure in general, a more holistic and systemic vision should be integrated for a *just and right* management of, on one side, all involved stakeholders, from primary to secondary ones, to non-human stakeholders, and of, on the other side, all generated socio-economic and environmental impacts – considering both the short and long-term scale – on the local or global environment and natural ecosystems. Hence, to move beyond the original concepts and definitions of Environmental Justice - i.e., ecological inequalities or the uneven distribution of environmental negative impacts, such as toxic waste, environmental pollution to poor, Latin, black or indigenous people – recent theories attempted to consider other dimensions and their relationships, or to expand the focus of the studies. For instance, the Critical Environmental Justice framework (Pellow, 2017) criticized the EJ original studies to focus solely on the institutional level and not on the power structure which generates such inequalities (Menton et al., 2020). According to Pellow (2017), for instance, Environmental Justice

---

[4] This last example will be discussed in detail in the next Chapters.

should emphasize the *intersectionality* among different sustainability dimensions (environmental, economic, social), adopt a *multi-scalar approach* (e.g. by including temporal and geographical dimensions), as well as adopt the *embeddedness* and *indispensability* principles, i.e., considering the complex interrelationships and causalities (*embeddedness*) among all non-substitutable (*indispensability*) human and non-human components of ecosystems. Similarly, the school of thought of Ecological Justice aims to expand the boundaries to all non-human entities, arguing that Environmental Justice is still anthropocentric and too focused on negative impact on humans (Kopnina & Washington, 2020).

Hence, to conclude this chapter and this discussion about environmental justice, in megaprojects and infrastructure projects' management it is crucial and fundamental to adopt a systemic, inclusive and expanded (toward non-human entities) vision and approach to manage stakeholders and impacts. In this sense, complex system theory (Hu et al., 2015) and system dynamics (Shams Esfandabadi et al., 2023) principles and approaches are of fundamental importance. For instance, by considering *balancing* and *reinforcing* feedback loops, i.e., closed (negative or positive) causalities loops, among different sustainability dimensions (social, economic, and environmental) and aspects, Shams Esfandabadi et al. (2023) showed how a bad management of, among other aspects, negative environmental impacts or health issues among workers and local population – for instance, induced by economic reasons to extract more value in the short-term from a construction infrastructure – generates a negative feedback loop in the long-term. In other terms, saving investments in the short-term may negatively affect megaproject's costs in the long-term due to the emergence and rise of social and environmental conflicts, which in certain cases may be avoided thanks to transparent and inclusive strategies, environmental impact assessment studies and stakeholder engagement processes. Indeed, as widely reported by the scientific literature on megaprojects, in the construction phase, protests and conflicts against the construction of a megaproject typically are provoked, among other factors, by environmental concerns and negative impacts, land expropriations, public services interruptions, corruption and/or the lack of a public debate (Bearfield & Dubnick, 2009; Corazza et al., 2022; Leung et al., 2013; Zucchetti et al., 2017). Thus, investment in measures to improve transparency, anti-corruption and impact accounting, health and safety of workers and the local population, to reduce environmental negative impacts (e.g., dusts, noises, greenhouse gas emissions, pollution, …), or to include actively local secondary stakeholders may minimize the emergence of environmental justice conflicts. Such a reduction effect can be understood, by adopting the terms of environmental sociology, in terms of the social metabolism (Padovan, 2000). Indeed, investing in such measures can be interpreted as a redistribution of the value that will be extracted to the local ecosystem (beyond mere economic compensation). In other words, the value generated in the long-term (no one of local communities or no entity of the local ecosystem will benefit from that value generated in the future) has to be redistributed and actualized today. It is clear that such an investment, in many cases where megaprojects and infrastructure are delayed for years or decades (think about the Turin-Lyon HSR, the Algarrobico hotel or the Notre-Dame-Des-Landes airport examples), is a required and positive investment strategy. Finally, inclusive and participatory stakeholder management strategies, with an ecosystem point of view (Kay et al., 1999), can also reduce the risk of social and environmental conflicts. What inclusive or systemic means and how it should look like will be discussed in detail in next chapters regarding the transnational megaproject of the Turin-Lyon high-speed railway line.

5.4. Summary

This chapter presents and introduces the environmental justice movements and some of the reasons behind social concerns and demonstrations against megaprojects. Drawing on a general historical discussion, starting from the Commons and the preservation and conservation of natural resources, this chapter interprets the social conflicts against megaprojects and infrastructure as an ecological distribution problem; in other words, conflicts against megaprojects may be generated and provoked (but not only) as a unjust redistribution of resources among generations (current affected population versus future users of the infrastructure), among local versus national/international communities and among public versus private profits and benefits. Finally, the chapter discusses a few relevant case studies from the Environmental Justice Atlas about large infrastructure, from new transportation hubs such as the new Notre-Dame-des-Landes airport in France or the Turin-Lyon high-speed railway in Italy, touristic facilities such as the illegal hotel in Algarrobico in Almeria in Spain or energy-related infrastructure such as the Trans Adriatic Pipeline in the South of Italy.

References

Algostino, A. (2016). The authoritarian approach of megaprojects versus democracy: the international people's court defends the right of participation. *Vision for Sustainability,* (5), 33-36.

Bearfield, D.A. & Dubnick, M.J. (2009). All mega-projects are local? Citizen participation lessons from the big dig. *Journal of Public Budgeting, Accounting & Financial Management*.

Bullard, R.D. (1996). Environmental Racism and the Environmental Justice Movement. In Cahn M.A. & O'Brien R. (Eds.), *Thinking About the environment. Readings on Politics, Property, and the Physical World*. Routledge Taylor & Francis Group.

Burballa-Noria, A. (2018). The case of the Forum Against Unnecessary and Imposed Megaprojects. In *The Right to Nature: Social Movements, Environmental Justice and Neoliberal Natures*. Routledge, 155–167.

Corazza, L., Torchia, D., Cottafava, D., Tipaldo, G. et al. (2022). Considering the social and economic implications of infrastructure megaprojects: theoretical contributions, practical challenges and managerial implications. In *The Impact of Corporate Social Responsibility. Corporate Activities, the Environment and Society*. Routledge, 1–30.

Ellena, M., Ballester, J., Mercogliano, P., Ferracin, E., Barbato, G., Costa, G. & Ingole, V. (2020). Social inequalities in heat-attributable mortality in the city of Turin, northwest of Italy: a time series analysis from 1982 to 2018. *Environmental Health: A Global Access Science Source*, 19(1), 1–14.

Ellena, M., Melis, G., Zengarini, N., Di Gangi, E., Ricciardi, G., Mercogliano, P. & Costa, G. (2023). Micro-scale UHI risk assessment on the heat-health nexus within cities by looking at socio-economic factors and built environment characteristics: The Turin case study (Italy). *Urban Climate*, 49(March).

Esposito, G., Nelson, T., Ferlie, E. & Crutzen, N. (2021). The institutional shaping of global megaprojects: The case of the Lyon-Turin high-speed railway. *International Journal of Project Management*, 39(6), 658–671.

Fischer Kowalski, M. & Haberl, H. (1997). Tons, joules, and money: Modes of production and their sustainability problems. *Society & Natural Resources*, 10(1), 61–85.

Fischer-Kowalski, M. & Haberl, H. (2015). Social metabolism: a metric for biophysical growth and degrowth. *Handbook of Ecological Economics*, 100–138.

Florez, M., Baudelle, G. & Hardouin, M. (2022). Notre-Dame-des-Landes or Redefining the Relationship to Space through the Territorial Embeddedness of a Struggle. *Antipode*, 54(3), 772–799.

Haas, W., Krausmann, F., Wiedenhofer, D. & Heinz, M. (2015). How circular is the global economy?: An assessment of material flows, waste production, and recycling in the European Union and the world in 2005. *Journal of Industrial Ecology*, 19(5), 765–777.

Hardin, G. (1968). The tragedy of the commons: the population problem has no technical solution; it requires a fundamental extension in morality. *Science, 162*(3859), 1243–1248.

Hardin, G. (1998). Extensions of "the tragedy of the commons". *Science, 280*(5364), 682–683.

Hardin, R. & Cullity, G. (2003). The free rider problem. *Stanford Encyclopedia of Philosophy.* https://plato.stanford.edu/entries/free-rider/.

Hu, Y., Chan, A.P.C., Le, Y. & Jin, R.-Z. (2015). From construction megaproject management to complex project management: Bibliographic analysis. *Journal of Management in Engineering, 31*(4).

Joan, M.-A. (1995). Distributional issues in ecological economics. *Review of Social Economy, 53*(4), 511–528.

Kay, J.J., Regier, H.A., Boyle, M. & Francis, G. (1999). An ecosystem approach for sustainability: addressing the challenge of complexity. *Futures, 31*(7), 721–742.

Kopnina, H. & Washington, H. (2020). Conservation and justice the Anthropocene: Definitions and debates. *Conservation: Integrating Social and Ecological Justice*, 3–15.

Leung, M., Yu, J. & Liang, Q. (2013). Improving public engagement in construction development projects from a stakeholder's perspective. *Journal of Construction Engineering and Management, 139*(11), 4013019.

Martinez-Alier, J. (2003). *The Environmentalism of the poor: a study of ecological conflicts and valuation*. Edward Elgar Publishing.

Martinez-Alier, J. & O'Connor, M. (1995). Ecological and economic distribution conflicts. In Costanza R., Segura, O. (Eds.), *Getting down to earth. Practical applications of ecological economics.* Island Press/ISEE.

Martinez-Alier, J., Temper, L., Del Bene, D. & Scheidel, A. (2016). Is there a global environmental justice movement? *Journal of Peasant Studies, 43*(3), 731–755.

Martinez-Alier, J., Temper, L. & Demaria, F. (2016). *Social metabolism and environmental conflicts in India*. Springer.

Mazzucato, M. (2018). *The value of everything: Making and taking in the global economy*. Hachette UK.

Melis, G., Di Gangi, E., Ellena, M., Zengarini, N., Ricciardi, G., Mercogliano, P. & Costa, G. (2023). Urban Heat Island effect and social vulnerability in Turin: Prioritizing climate change mitigation action with an equity perspective. *Science Talks, 8*(May), 100258.

Menton, M., Larrea, C., Latorre, S., Martinez-Alier, J., Peck, M., Temper, L. & Walter, M. (2020). Environmental justice and the SDGs: from synergies to gaps and contradictions. *Sustainability Science, 15*(6), 1621–1636.

Nixon, R. (2011). *Slow Violence and the Environmentalism of the Poor.* Harvard University Press.

Ostrom, E. (1990). *Governing the commons: The evolution of institutions for collective action*. Cambridge University Press.

Padovan, D. (2000). The concept of social metabolism in classical sociology. *Theomai, 2*.

Pellow, D.N. (2017). *What is critical environmental justice?* John Wiley & Sons.

Rawls, J. (1996). The Problem of Justice Between Generations. In Cahn, M.A. & O'Brien, R. (Eds.), *Thinking About the environment. Readings on Politics, Property, and the Physical World*. Routledge. Taylor & Francis Group.

Rifkin, J. (2014). *The zero marginal cost society: The internet of things, the collaborative commons, and the eclipse of capitalism*. Macmillan, Palgrave.

Rose, C. (1986). The comedy of the commons: custom, commerce, and inherently public property. *The University of Chicago Law Review, 53*(3), 711–781.

Shams Esfandabadi, Z., Cottafava, D., Corazza, L. & Scagnelli, S.D. (2023). Sustainability Challenges of High-speed Railway Megaprojects from a Systems Thinking Lens. *Complexity and Sustainability in Megaprojects*, (June).

Staglianò, R. (2016). Il tram che fa perdere cinque mesi di vita al chilometro. *La Repubblica*. https://www.repubblica.it/venerdi/reportage/2016/06/06/news/sul_tram_che_ti_dice_quanto_vivrai-141429480/.

Tarrow, S. (2005). *The new transnational activism*. Cambridge University Press.

Temper, L., Bene, D. del & Martinez-Alier, J. (2015). Mapping the frontiers and front lines of global environmental justice: The EJAtlas. *Journal of Political Ecology, 22*(266642), 254–278.

Temper, L., Demaria, F., Scheidel, A., Del Bene, D. & Martinez-Alier, J. (2018). The Global Environmental Justice Atlas (EJAtlas): ecological distribution conflicts as forces for sustainability. *Sustainability Science, 13*(3), 573–584.

The European Parliament and the Council. (2013). Regulation (EU) No 1315/2013 of the European Parliament AND OF THE Council of 11 December 2013 on Union guidelines for the development of the trans-European transport network and repealing Decision No 661/2010/EU. *Official Journal of the European Union*. https://eur-lex.europa.eu/homepage.html.

Wenz, P. (1996). Environmental Justice. In Cahn, M.A. & O'Brien, R. (Eds.), *Thinking About the environment. Readings on Politics, Property, and the Physical World*. Routledge Taylor & Francis Group.

Zidane, Y.J.T., Hussein, B.A., Johansen, A. & Andersen, B. (2016).

PESTOL-framework for «project evaluation on strategic, tactical and operational levels». *International Journal of Information Systems and Project Management*, 4(3), 25–41.

Zucchetti, M., Clerico, M., Giunti, L., Mercalli, L., Poggio, A., Ponti, M., Tartaglia, A. & Ulgiati, S. (2017). The Turin-lyon high-speed rail: A technical assessment. *International Journal of Ecosystems & Ecology Sciences*, 7(1).

Chapter 6

A HISTORICAL AND EMPIRICAL ANALYSIS OF STAKEHOLDERS IN THE TURIN-LYON RAILWAY LINE: TOWARDS AN INCLUSIVE AND ECOSYSTEMIC VISION OF STAKEHOLDER MANAGEMENT

ABSTRACT: *This chapter provides a historical reconstruction of the events that led the Turin-Lyon High Speed Rail megaproject to become one of the most contested projects in Europe. Then, by embracing a relational approach to stakeholder engagement, which also takes MSR into account, it provides an empirical analysis of the stakeholder ecosystem of this project. Qualitative and quantitative research is conducted to reconstruct the stakeholder networks from the perspective of managers and directors of TELT, the company serving as the public promoter for the megaproject. It is argued that the understanding and prioritization of stakeholders is still geared mostly toward internal and national and supranational institutional stakeholder, rather than including firmly local communities and institutions.*

SUMMARY: 6.1. Introduction. – 6.2. A short history of the Turin-Lyon high speed rail. – 6.3. Methodology. – 6.4. Results. – 6.5. Summary. – *References*.

6.1. Introduction

Chapter 2 of this book has focused on the evolution of stakeholder theory for megaprojects and how the adoption of a relational stakeholder approach (Rowley, 2017) could facilitate the transition towards sustainable megaproject management, incorporating the principles of megaproject social responsibility (MSR). This chapter builds on this to analyze empirically one of the most controversial and contested megaprojects in Italy (and Europe), the Turin-Lyon High Speed Railway (HSR) line, or simply TAV (from the Italian "Treno Alta Velocità"). From a European perspective, the new railway line is a key part of the EU program to develop the Trans-European Transport Network (TEN-T), which includes 9 corridors to connect the entire continent quickly, efficiently, and sustainably. The Turin-Lyon line will be 270 km long, with a 65 km cross-border section featuring the longest tunnel in the world, 57.5 km between the Susa Valley in Italy and the Maurienne Valley (of which 12.5 in Italy and 45 in France), as part of the Mediterranean Corridor. The cross-border section is certainly the most interesting part of the megaproject, as well as the most expensive. In 2012, the project for the cross-border section of the line received a cost certification by a third party of €8.3bln, which rises to €9.6bln in today's currency. In terms of funding, the section is funded by the European Union for 40% (with good chances of increasing the share to 50%), by Italy for 35%, and by France for 25% (TELT, 2023).

From a stakeholder perspective, the project has a long history of communication and inclusion issues, which have led to a polarization of opinions, from local governments to citizens, and a strenuous resistance to the construction of this new line that has even spurred a long series of episodes of violence and fights between protestors and armed forces. This case shows how complicated managing stakeholder relations in megaprojects is, especially because there are different levels of actors involved, constituting therefore a network of networks. This chapter presents a mixed-methods primary research: the qualitative part discusses how managers and directors of TELT, the company serving as the public promoter of the Turin-Lyon railway line, understand and classify the stakeholders involved in the project; the quantitative part aims first to develop an applied methodology to visualize and understand stakeholder networks, by using Social Network Analysis (SNA) and then, by mapping how stakeholders are connected, to devise operational ways to manage stakeholders' interests. This research strives therefore to move beyond a purely firm-centric approach in stakeholder management, as advocated by Rowley (1997). As opposed to the concept of stakeholder salience, this chapter shows that a wise and effective stakeholder management should be influenced by the nature and intensity of the relationships developed within the megaproject as a whole. This leads to moral and ethical considerations on how stakeholder's interests should be managed, especially in the complex dynamics surrounding a megaproject in which, for example, local residents should be included among the relevant actors.

6.2. A short history of the Turin-Lyon high speed rail

The Turin-Lyon HSR line is a megaproject that, despite being still far from completion, has already gotten over thirty years of history. Its origins can be traced back to the end of the 1980s, when prominent industrial figures of Turin, under the name of *Associazione Tecnocity*, presented the very first proposal of a high-speed railway line in a public conference organized by *Fondazione Agnelli*. Around the same time, SNCF, the French national railway company, suggested that the existing line could have been replaced by a newer and more efficient one, which could provide better connections and efficiently support industrial exchanges between France and Italy (Esposito et al., 2020). Shortly after in Italy, capitalizing on the success of the first proposal, high-profile representatives of the industrial and political scene of Turin and the Piedmont region, led by Umberto Agnelli and Vittorio Beltrami, formed the *Comitato Promotore per l'Alta Velocità*[1] in 1990, to stress the importance of the megaproject (Manfredi et al., 2015). Being backed up by local institutions from the beginning, the committee was soon able to spark interest in the Italian government and, already in 1991, the idea was also appreciated by the leadership of *Ferrovie dello Stato Italiane* (FSI), the state-owned company managing both the infrastructure and services on the Italian rail network. While the enthusiasm for the potential benefits of the new line for the industry came initially from France, both countries believed that this megaproject could create sustainable transportation, reducing carbon emissions, and favoring this type of mobility over more environmentally impacting ones. Moreover, it was believed that it could lead to improving the economy, creating jobs, reducing traffic and, consequently, saving time (Marincioni & Appiotti, 2009).

As reported by Manfredi et al. (2015), not everybody was thrilled by the proposal, and some people manifested diffidence and dissent over the utility of the line, especially local institutions and civil society in the Susa Valley, the Italian valley in the Piedmontese Alps where the megaproject would be located. However, the situation was not the same in France and Italy. On the one hand, France had already introduced legal measures to increase stakeholder participation and acceptance in the 1990s, such as the *Loi Barnier* in 1995 towards environmental protection, and also created the *Commission Nationale du Débat Public* (CNPD), an independent administrative authority aimed at ensuring transparent and impartial debates (Burnside-Lawry & Ariemma, 2015). The French institutions and SNCF organized informative meetings in 1992–93 with the local communities, in the form of a *débat public*, where different aspects of the projects, supported by studies were presented to the population, which in turn could voice their concerns (Esposito et al., 2020). On the other hand, (especially) residents of the Susa Valley in Italy complained that the Italian national government managed the planning phase of the megaproject without properly

---

[1] The Committee included a variety of stakeholders like FIAT, Olivetti, The Industrial Union of Turin, The Turin Chamber of Commerce, Confindustria Piemonte, Unioncamere, Piemonte, San Paolo IMI Bank, as well as the Municipality of Turin and the Province of Turin (Manfredi et al, p. 3).

involving local institutions and communities, leveraging on the laws contained within the *Strategic Infrastructure Act*. For local residents this signaled a lack of power and consideration as stakeholders (Marincioni & Appiotti, 2009). The residents of the valley were mostly concerned about the environmental and socioeconomic implications of the megaproject, and their feelings were heightened by the impotence they felt. From an environmental point of view, it was pointed out the risk of uranium and asbestos release during excavations of the surrounding mountains (Fornero et al., 2005), along with increasing noise and pollution in the valley. On top of everything else, many stressed that life in the valley would have been impacted for over a decade, for the presence of construction sites operating in the area. The proposed line was also harshly condemned for the high costs linked to it, especially in light of its goals of better managing increasing traffic flows between the two countries, while critics pointed out that such flows were instead declining over time (Armano et al., 2013; Esposito et al., 2020).

It is argued that environmental concerns soon became mixed with a sense of cultural resistance to the relentless advancing of globalization, sparking the birth of the No TAV ("No Treno Alta Velocità", meaning No High-Speed Rail) movement in Italy (Leonardi, 2013). The No TAV movement is very heterogeneous, including local institutions, citizens, academics, technical experts, as well as violent fringe groups. Leonardi (2013) sees the No TAV movement as a space for new and alternative forms of organizing and self-governance, rather than something that just goes against the status quo.

The next step was the formation of the company *Alpentunnel*, which conducted feasibility studies, making way for the joint agreement between the Italian and French governments in 2001 and the consequent setting up of the binational company *Lyon-Turin Ferroviaire* (LTF), as an equal partnership between *Rete Ferroviaria Italiana* (RFI) and *Réseau Ferrè de France* (RFF). The first operational steps consisted in excavations in France and expropriations in Italy. Italian residents manifested preoccupation when LTF showed a project to excavate an exploratory tunnel in Venaus, a small town in the Susa Valley, fearing that asbestos could have been released.

In the early 2000s, the different situation between Italy and France became even more apparent. In France the *débat public* continued fruitfully, also thanks to the work of the independent experts that formed the *Commission d'Enquête Publique*. The commission produced a report for the government on the project after consulting local citizens, who brought to the fore environmental concerns and led the government to conduct a new public enquiry in the town where such concerns were raised (Esposito et al., 2020). Moreover, in 2003, the French government, through the *Comité Interministériel d'Aménagement et de Développement du Territoire* (CIADT) decided that the Turin-Lyon megaproject was to benefit from the *démarche Grand Chantier*, which concerns in particular employment, training, housing, support to the economic fabric and local development in the Maurienne Valley. As reported by TELT (2023), between 2002 and 2010, the *demarche* made it possible to hire between 40 and 50% of people originating from the Rhône-Alpes Region, of which about 30% from Savoy, to be employed in the Maurienne construction sites.

In Italy instead, the conflict escalated quickly, with fringes of the No TAV movement manifesting resistance in the winter of 2005, ultimately leading to militarization in the valley and of the construction sites. The occupation of the sites by over 30,000 supporters of the movement in December 2005, convinced the government to adopt a different strategy that did not include Venaus. This state of crisis led the Italian government to look for a mediation and set up the *Institutional Forum of Palazzo Chigi* to mostly negotiate among institutions at different levels, and the *Technical Observatory* to favor dialogue among different parties and stakeholders on several issues. The *Observatory* was made of governmental representatives, local authorities, and representatives of RFI and LTF, with Mario Virano as President (who will later become TELT's General Director). The *Observatory* admitted the many communication and inclusion mistakes made in the past, which left many stakeholders feeling neglected. The *Observatory* conducted 300 audits in its first year, but many proposals were still met with diffidence, while time was inexorably passing by, leaving the proponents with little time to devise a new project, and avoiding losing the EU funding (Manfredi et al., 2015). While the relationship between the *Observatory* and local authorities got strained once it became known that in the funding request to the EU there was a proposed new route that had not been discussed with all the parties (Debernardi & Grimaldi, 2012), by the end of 2007 the funding was approved.

As the project moved forward, the *Observatory* got closer to becoming a governance body, rather than a discussion forum for stakeholders, causing further dissent on its role and usefulness (Ariemma & Burnside-Lawry, 2011). Drilling finally began in 2009, and the following year Chiomonte, a town in the Susa Valley, was chosen as the main construction site. Shortly after, the definitive project for the exploratory tunnel La Maddalena (located in Chiomonte), was approved, again under threats from the EU of withdrawing funding for the project. When the site was opened in 2011, a new series of protests were made by the No TAV movement, and the area surrounding the construction site was occupied. The protestors set up the *Free*

Republic of the Maddalena (Auriemma & Burnside-Lawry, 2011), leading to a long conflict with the police and the military forces, at the end of which the rioters were evacuated. This resulted in a further militarization of the site, which was also put under continuous surveillance (Burnside-Lawry & Ariemma, 2015), and still is to date.

In 2012 the two governments signed an agreement to define what the functions, structure and responsibilities should be, including issues like procurements, costs, and compensations to the towns involved. *Tunnel Euralpin Lyon Turin* (TELT) was created in 2015, replacing LTF, to mainly bring the tunnel to fruition. In 2017 it was finally decided that the excavation tunnel would have been done in Chiomonte. However, the project came to a new halt in 2018, when the newly installed Italian government, through the *Ministry of Infrastructure and Transport* demanded a new Cost-Benefit Analysis, which followed the one done in 2011, but this time externally run by the economist Marco Ponti. The results of the analysis showed a potentially negative return on investment (Esposito et al., 2020), with a negative net value between 6 and 8 billion € (then revised to 3.5), but the Italian government decided to carry on with the project anyway. The reasons behind this decision, despite the negative outcome of the Cost-Benefit Analysis must be found in the willingness for the EU to increase its funding for the project, and at the same time motivated by the fear of losing such funds, in case of other delays that the EU would not appreciate, considering the importance of the project in developing the Mediterranean Corridor. At the end of 2019, TELT started sending work specifications to construction companies for the works on the French side and for the realization of interchange niches in the geognostic tunnel of Chiomonte (Wick, 2020).

Following a period of relative stability, in 2020 protests and rallies restarted in the Susa Valley. Several clashes took place in the following years (2021–23) in the small town of San Didero, in the area where the new truck terminal will be built, in place of the old one located just 20 km away, in Susa, signaling that the flame of resistance is still burning. On the operational side, works are underway and, at the time of writing (September 2023) a big contract worth €1 billion for the excavation of the base tunnel in Italy was assigned, along with smaller tenders both in Italy and in France, while a €3 billion tender for the railway and technological equipment and maintenance of the international section of the Turin-Lyon railway line is currently ongoing.

6.3. Methodology

As said earlier in this chapter and elsewhere in the book, an increasing number of scholars are supportive of the relational view of stakeholder theory, but it still lacks empirical evidence of its applicability. This gap can be partly filled by using SNA tools to visually represent stakeholder relationships and networks (Rowley, 2017). This research can be classified as mixed methods (Johnson and Onweugbuzie, 2004), including both qualitative and quantitative parts. To prepare for the SNA, 21 semi-structured interviews and a focus group were conducted with TELT's managers and directors, in which respondents were asked to identify the project stakeholders from their perspective. This process highlighted the different relationships that managers in different positions and roles have developed with the internal and external environment. The following step, aimed at reconstructing the ecosystem of relations, as advocated by Rowley (1997, 2017), consisted in a quantitative analysis based on the centrality degrees to test what prioritization techniques were used to address stakeholders' issues. To this end, building on Sayer et al. (2023), the use of a SNA aims at creating knowledge on how stakeholders are managed in complex and highly contentious environments. Data from the qualitative research were used to create the stakeholder network, starting with a snowballing sampling based on the interviewees. Basically, each node of the network corresponds to a stakeholder listed by the respondents, while the connecting links, representing the different relations among the actors (interviewees and identified stakeholders), were assigned when relations between two nodes were outlined by the interviewees. Following a process of homogenization of names and categories, the single snowball networks resulting from each interview were combined into a single network. This can be defined as a bottom-up mapping process, due to the direct engagement of primary internal stakeholders. Finally, an analysis of the centrality degree was performed over the whole network to point out an "emergent" prioritization of stakeholders. Emergent, using complex system terminology, means a property and feature that can be revealed only by analyzing the whole network and stakeholders' ecosystem. The resulting full stakeholder network was analyzed with the Gephi software, thanks to four centrality degree indicators: 1 – authority (Kleinberg, 1999); 2 – PageRank (Brin & Page, 1998); 3 – eigenvector (Segarra & Ribeiro, 2014); 4 – betweenness (Freeman, 1977; Brandes, 2001). The former three indicators measured, although with some differences, the importance of a node with respect to the first and second-order neighbors (i.e., evaluating the centrality of a node over the whole network but weighting it with respect to the centrality of its neighborhood), while the latter, namely the betweenness, measures the number of shortest paths between any couple of nodes of the network passing through the analyzed node. In other words, it measures the ability of a node to act as a bridge and connector within the entire network. Regarding the methodology, it must be highlighted that, as the data represent the network of actors from the perspective of the interviewees, all working for TELT, the resulting picture only reflects how such managers and directors construct their relations, rather than the full stakeholder ecosystem.

6.4. Results

The qualitative part of the study reveals interesting results in how stakeholders are understood and defined. With some important exceptions, generally the more institutional figures in the company tend to have a broader vision of the stakeholders involved than operational managers. For instance, one director argues that *'we have a robust set of stakeholders, of whom we cannot do without to run the project. And these are basically all the territorial stakeholders. So, the first stakeholders, the first people to whom we are accountable are the local communities'*. While a certain openness to an inclusive stakeholder approach is more common among directors, one site manager also expresses that *'every citizen is a stakeholder including, perhaps, those who will be using the line in the future'*. Building on this and reflecting on the troubled path that the megaproject has had over the years, another director states that *'all parties, all causes, must be considered equally important. We witnessed that all stakes, facts and needs, up to a micro scale, in reality bear effects and influence matters of primary importance'*.

Other respondents, especially site managers, instead manifest a narrower and more limited definition of their stakeholder network, including mostly internal stakeholders to the company. One argues that *'we (TELT) are the real stakeholders, because we are the ones called to do the tunnel. So, for me the stakeholders are those who make the realization of the works possible'*. Another says that *'the most important actors are the construction companies and work direction, while the other actors are more like second level'*. Another site manager sees stakeholders mainly along two dimensions, those who want to do the megaproject and those who are monitoring the environment: *'my definition is as an internal stakeholder. The overriding interest is to combine environmental aspects and the implementation of the work, so finding a falling point that brings together these interests that are typically conflicting'*.

To sum up the qualitative results from the interviews, despite the longstanding history of conflict and resistance, several respondents still adopt a stakeholder vision that is rather limited to those who surround the construction and management of the project, which is accentuated by the often-practical role that interviewees have in the construction operations. However, the longer respondents have been involved in the project and are embedded in the territories (family roots, personal connections to the community, political involvement), the more they tend to have a broader encompassing vision.

In the quantitative part of the research a stakeholder mapping was conducted by extrapolating from interviews when an actor was mentioned, resulting in the identification of 95 stakeholder groups and over 360 relations. The actors represented belong to several groups, including the public administration at supranational, national and local level; the third sector; private companies, mostly in activities related to the construction of the megaproject, and finally managerial units internal to the company. The SNA identified five different clusters: civil society; internal and external project stakeholders; national governments and the EU; national governmental bodies (like ministries), and local institutions. Regarding the centrality degrees, instead, while PageRank focuses mainly on national and international public institutions as well as certain civil society components that represent generic construction and engineering companies, Authority is primarily attributable to national and international public institutions. In terms of their authority, public environmental institutions like the Ministry of Environment and Arpa Piemonte, which is in charge of confirming the environmental quality assessment on all construction sites, are more central. Finally, internal business units are the primary focus of the betweenness centrality. This outcome stems from the organization-centered interviews (i.e., only director and internal managers were engaged), and as a result has limited relevance.

Therefore, excluding the Betweenness centrality, whose results were biased, the Authority, PageRank and EigenVector centrality degrees showed that, with some variations among them, the social components emerging from the network constructed from the interviews appear less relevant than the internal stakeholders and national and international institutions. This demonstrated how the managers' perception of the stakeholders' network, as emerged and declared from the interviews (i.e., from the qualitative analysis), was partially in contrast with the findings obtained from the Social Network Analysis and the centrality degrees (i.e., from the quantitative analysis). Concluding, if on one side, interviews are useful to reveal the inner behavior of managers (e.g., their idea of most relevant and important stakeholders), on the other side, the SNA is a useful tool to highlight the real consequence of their actions with an ecosystem point of view, overcoming a firm-centric stakeholder analysis. Therefore, the SNA can be a very useful tool to help managers and directors to be more aware of external stakeholders and of the influence they carry on the project.

6.5. Summary

This chapter has analyzed the history of the Turin-Lyon high speed railway line. It highlighted the difficulties, especially on the Italian side, to fix early communication and inclusion issues towards local residents and institutions, which have led to a strong polarization of opinions that resulted in resistance and several and prolonged episodes of violence. Embracing a relational approach to stakeholder management, the chapter also presented results from a mixed-methods primary research conducted on managers and directors of TELT, the public promoter of the project. Both the interviews and the SNA conducted showed that, despite a general awareness of the stakeholder ecosystem, for the most part, respondents found closeness to those stakeholders directly relevant to their function and role. This showed that a relational and inclusive understanding of stakeholders is yet to be fully achieved, and that the project is likely to still suffer from its troubled past and from the differences in how local stakeholders have been managed in the two countries.

References

Aaltonen, K. (2011). Project stakeholder analysis as an environmental interpretation process. *International journal of project management*, 29(2), 165–183.

Ariemma, L. & Burnside-Lawry, J. (2016). Transnational resistance networks: New democratic prospects? The Lyon-Turin railway and no TAV movement. In *Protest, social movements and global democracy since 2011: New perspectives*. Vol. 39. Emerald Group Publishing Limited, 137–165.

Armano, E., Pittavino, G.L. & Sciortino, R. (2013). Occupy in Valsusa: the No TAV movement. *Capitalism Nature Socialism*, 24(2), 14–26.

Brandes, U. (2001). A faster algorithm for betweenness centrality. *Journal of mathematical sociology*, 25(2), 163–177.

Brin, S. & Page, L. (1998). The anatomy of a large-scale hypertextual web search engine. *Computer networks and ISDN systems*, 30(1–7), 107–117.

Burnside-Lawry, J. & Ariemma, L. (2015). Global governance and communicative action: a study of democratic participation during planning for the Lyon–Turin rail link. *Journal of Public Affairs*, 15(2), 129–142.

Debernardi, A. & Grimaldi, R. (2012). La nuova linea Torino-Lione. In *C'è luce in fondo al tunnel? Analisi e spunti sulle politiche infrastrutturali ferroviarie alpine*, 129–178. Maggioli Editore.

Esposito, G., Terlizzi, A. & Crutzen, N. (2022). Policy narratives and megaprojects: The case of the Lyon-Turin high-speed railway. *Public Management Review*, 24(1), 55–79.

Fornero, E., Bellis, D., Tomatis, M., Bruna, L., Piazzano, P., Schellino, G., Belluso, E. & Fubini, B. (2005). A cattle model of environmental exposure to asbestos in Lanzo and Susa valleys (Piedmont region): possible fiber accumulation mechanism in cow lungs. [Review of A cattle model of environmental exposure to asbestos in Lanzo and Susa valleys (Piedmont region): possible fiber accumulation mechanism in cow lungs]. In *International Conference on Asbestos Monitoring and Analytical Methods - AMAM 2005, Book of abstracts*. Ca' Foscari University of Venice.

Freeman, L.C. (1977). A set of measures of centrality based on betweenness. *Sociometry*, 35–41.

Kleinberg, J.M. (1999). Hubs, authorities, and communities. *ACM computing surveys (CSUR)*, 31(4es), 5-es.

Leonardi, E. (2013). Foucault in the Susa Valley: the NO TAV movement and struggles for Subjectification. *Capitalism Nature Socialism*, 24(2), 27–40.

Manfredi, P., Massarente, C., Violet, F., Cannarsa, M., Mazza, C. & Ferraris, V. (2015). *A Brief History of Turin-Lyon High-Speed Railway*, 1–16. http://www.warningoncrime.eu/wpcontent/uploads/2015/12/ws2_tav_history.pdf.

Marincioni, F. & Appiotti, F. (2009). The Lyon-Turin high-speed rail: the public debate and perception of environmental risk in Susa valley, Italy. *Environmental management*, 43, 863–875.

Rowley, T.J. (1997). Moving beyond dyadic ties: A network theory of stakeholder influences. *Academy of management Review*, 22(4), 887–910.

Rowley, T.J. (2017). The power of and in stakeholder networks. In Wasieleski, D.M. & Weber, J. (Eds.), *Business and Society 360*. Vol. 1. Emerald Publishing Limited, 101–122.

Sayer, B., Dumay, J., Guthrie, J. & Corazza, L. (2023). *Making Sense of Stakeholder Management*. Taylor & Francis.

Segarra, S. & Ribeiro, A. (2015). Stability and continuity of centrality measures in weighted graphs. *IEEE Transactions on Signal Processing*, 64(3), 543–555.

TELT (2023). *Partnerships.* https://www.telt.eu/en/telt-public-promoter/a-european-partnership/.
TELT (2023). *Torino – Lione beneficia del Démarche Grand Chantier.* https://www.telt.eu/it/torino-lione-beneficia-del-demarche-grand-chantier/.
Wijck, A. von (2020). *Lyon-Turin begins base line tender process.* https://www.tunneltalk.com/Lyon-Turin-19Mar2020-major-contracts-for-Lyon-Turin-base-tunnel.php.

Chapter 7

BETWEEN SUSTAINABILITY AND SOCIAL INNOVATION: THE IMPORTANCE OF THE LOCAL IDENTITY AND COMMUNITIES

ABSTRACT: *This chapter focuses on recent forms of neo-rural entrepreneurship in the Susa Valley (Alpine Valley) relying on the debate about the new "centrality" of the mountain areas, a discourse that can be placed at the intersection of different local development interpretative models in which the traditional urban-centric perception of mountain territories, traditionally described as "intermediate" or "marginal" territories has weakened. In particular, the analysis will focus on 1. the conditions that allowed new forms of entrepreneurship in the Susa Valley, as well as the critical issues that hindered the establishment and development of new entrepreneurial paths, 2. the local identity, 3. the Turin-Lyon HSR case, 4. the metro-mountain connections, 5. the life and work experience of new "entrepreneurs-mountaineers".*

SUMMARY: 7.1. Introduction. – 7.2. Background. – 7.2.1. The crisis of the center-periphery model: the complexity and new strategic centrality of mountain and metro-mountain areas. – 7.2.2. A hybrid mountain: the case of the Susa Valley. – 7.2.3. A new institutional perspective to overcome the "marginality" of places. – 7.3. Methodology. – 7.4. Results and findings. – 7.4.1. A "responsible" ecosystem with a strong identity. – 7.5. Conclusions. – 7.6. Summary. – *References*.

7.1. Introduction

The increasing scrutiny of a model founded upon a robust center-periphery dichotomy highlights a growing impracticality. Recent studies have begun to highlight the significance of peripheries, which are no longer considered negligible in the context of local development. The debate on the new "centrality" of mountain areas can be placed at the intersection of different local development interpretative models, in which the traditional urban-centric perception of mountain territories, traditionally described as "*intermediate*" or "*marginal*" (Bonomi, 2013), has weakened. The dichotomous perspective that has pitted Italian "*marginal*" mountains against urban places of "*modernity and development*", now conveys the need to refocus on the territories at the margin (De Rossi, 2018, p. 14). This is due to a number of reasons: first of all, Italy is so surrounded with mountain territories such that this should be considered a national issue that cannot be treated in a residual manner (De Rossi, 2018; Barbera & De Rossi, 2021); secondly, because in this proposal there are cultural, social and economic reasons that lead us to reconsider the Alpine and Apennine areas as potential places of economic and social innovation. In this regard, the research presented herein has been conducted in 2020 and 2021 and it highlights, *inter alia*, new forms of entrepreneurship and social innovation practices in the mountain and metro-mountain territories of the Susa Valley, the same place where the Turin-Lyon megaproject is impacting.

The rest of the chapter is structured as follows. The first section deals with the center-periphery model, its critical aspects and the theme of the new centrality of mountain and metro-mountain areas, following three main research fields: the traditional literature on local development, parallel studies in the geographic-sociological fields related to the development paths of the metro-mountain areas and social innovation studies. We examine the case of the Susa Valley by referring to a review of the literature on the different taxonomic proposals for the description of the valley. Then, we present our qualitative research, aimed at identifying and analyzing 1. the conditions that allow new forms of entrepreneurship in the Susa Valley, as well as the critical issues that hinder the establishment and development of new entrepreneurial paths; 2. the local identity; 3. the Turin-Lyon HSR case; 4. the metro-mountain connections; 5. the life and work experience of new "entrepreneurs- mountaineers".

Drawing on the analysis of neo-rural forms of entrepreneurship and of best entrepreneurial practices in the field of social innovation, our study in section 7.4.1. reveals a significant and emergent link among the concepts of sustainability,[1] social innovation and local development in marginal areas. This study is therefore an attempt to shed light on the mountain area's identity and on the phenomenon of neo-ruralism and its local effects in socio-economic terms, as well as on the importance of the inclusion of the local community in the decision-making processes related to megaprojects (specifically to the Turin-Lyon HSR).

7.2. Background

In the following sections, we deal with the literature that inspired the analysis of the Susa Valley case study. In section 7.2.1 we address a part of local development literature that deals with mountain and metro-mountain areas; in section 7.2.2 we discuss the issue of the heterogeneity of the mountain territories, referring to the case of the Susa Valley, and in the last section we treat the issue of marginality of places and the consequences arising

---

[1] With this term, we mainly refer to the corporate and institutional "responsible" practices, or those attributable to the concept of corporate social responsibility (CSR).

from the exclusion of these places and their communities from institutional decision-making processes.

7.2.1. The crisis of the center-periphery model: the complexity and new strategic centrality of mountain and metro-mountain areas

The large body of literature dealing with local development intersects economic, sociological and geographical contributions that since the 1970s have begun to question a dominant economic paradigm centered on the dualistic interpretative proposal that, in the Italian case, it simply counterposed an industrialized North to an agricultural South, an urban and productive center to an agricultural or little industrialized periphery (Lutz, 1958). Among these, the proposal of Bagnasco (1977) and of Becattini (1978, 1989) invited to a re-reading of economic phenomena as intertwined and dependent on cultural, social and historical aspects attributable to a certain territory, as a result of a historical path shared by a community of people. In the ideal case, this aspect is typical of the districts of Third Italy,[2] with local productive specializations based on geographical, cultural and institutional proximity, but also on the strength of the social ties embedded in specific areas. Starting from these paradigmatic contributions, empirical research in the following years (Trigilia, 2005; Becattini, 2001, 2015) shed light on the complexity of this "kaleidoscopic" variety characterizing the different local development paths in Italy.

The debate on the new *centrality* of the mountain areas can be placed at the intersection of different local development interpretative models and in a change of paradigm occurred at the institutional level, where in the last decade the need to adopt a place-based approach (Barca et al., 2012) for the policies of socio-economic development has incentivized different institutional measures. For instance, in 2013 the Italian government approved the so-called *National Strategy for Inner Areas* (SNAI). SNAI is a policy framework aimed at addressing the economic and social challenges faced by the country's internal or inland areas. The strategy was developed to promote sustainable development, reduce regional disparities, and improve the quality of life in these areas. With this intent, SNAI provides guidelines on economic development, infrastructure and services, cultural and environmental assets, social inclusion and territorial governance. It takes up the lesson of active planning, in order to accelerate or induce processes of

---

[2] The term "Third Italy" was coined by Arnaldo Bagnasco (1977) to refer to the areas of north-eastern and central Italy characterized by the strong presence of crafts-based small firms, clustered in a constellation of specialized industrial districts.

change towards new development paths of post-industrial transition. SNAI's ultimate goals are towards a formulation of local development projects that concern the active and sustainable protection of the territory, the enhancement of natural and cultural capital, tourism, agri-food industry, local know-how and craftsmanship, supply of essential services, as well as the activation of renewable energy supply chains. These macro-objectives are to be pursued through intermediate objectives such as: increasing the well-being of the local population and the local demand for labor and employment, increasing the degree of utilization of territorial capital, reducing the social costs of de-anthropization, and strengthening the local development factors (MIUR, 2013).

In this perspective, with the use of the word "*metro-mountain*", scholars of local development policies mean the strengthening of cultural and operative connections between the mountain and the city, aimed at deconstructing the city-mountain dichotomy, with the purpose of emphasizing a polycentric development in line with the territorial and cultural diversity of Italy, its resources and the latent and unexpressed potential of the "*middle spaces*", traditionally described as "*intermediate*" or "*marginal*" territories (Bonomi, 2013). The notion of *metro-mountain areas* stems from these foundational principles and from a pragmatic understanding that the future context cannot be based on a perspective of infinite growth. Moreover, the *aims* of the ecological transition require a change of mentality for which the mountain's territorial capital must be maintained, reinterpreted, reused and innovated (Barbera & De Rossi, 2021). It is in this u-turn (Membretti, 2021), within this change of academic and institutional perspective on the role and value of the mountain that the analysis of forms of neo-ruralism and innovative entrepreneurship must be contextualized. This should also include the experience of the so-called "*new mountaineers*" (Corrado et al., 2014; Barbera et al., 2019), i.e., that of "*mountaineers by choice*", subjects who voluntarily leave the urban-metropolitan areas, choosing to live and work in the mountains.

Living in the mountains as a life choice is usually explained as a healthier and more balanced lifestyle, or as an option for those who want to start their own businesses in areas like farming, forestry, tourism, and personal services. These businesses often blend agriculture and tourism, offering sustainable and circular economic practices. This helps change the traditional perception of mountains as tourist destinations to places where innovation and socio-economic development can help the local economy thrive. Indeed, these small businesses and self-entrepreneurs certainly contribute to reverse the stereotypical and conservative image of the mountain as a place whose vocation is exquisitely that of tourism, towards that of a potential place of innovation and socio-economic development (Barbera et al., 2019).

The image and perception of the mountain therefore oscillates between *"regressive"* aspects, which identify the mountain only as cultural and natural resources, and the dynamism of territorial marketing strategies sponsoring new forms of entrepreneurship and local development (De Rossi, 2018; Barbera & De Rossi, 2021). In a word, there is no more space for dualism such as centers-suburbs, North-South and city-country but, on the contrary, there is an ever-increasing complexity of hybrid, contradictory and dynamic aspects, where the boundaries are less clear and more fluid (Cersosimo et al., 2018). With this in mind, it appears clear how important it is to embrace the analysis addressing the new features of post-metropolitan (Balducci et al., 2017) and metro-mountain areas.

7.2.2. A hybrid mountain: the case of the Susa Valley

The Susa Valley is a suitable case to highlight the complexity of the mountain areas, characterized by the coexistence of urban settings, metro-mountain and mountain areas. From the historical, anthropological and productive viewpoint, the Susa Valley can be conceived as an *unicum* that embeds two territories marked by a different development path: the upper and lower valley. This distinction is not only linked to the orographic characteristics but it is instead referred to two different and complementary models of socio-economic development. Some authors describe the valley as an *"extraordinary mix between business factories and mountain"*, where the lower valley, characterized mostly by an industrial environment, was flanked by the agro-pastoral reality of the upper valley (Aime, 2016, p. 34). This description stresses an effective image of the prevailing bi-vocation that has long characterized the economy of the territory.

In the lower valley, a process of anticipated industrialization took place in the mid-nineteenth century, mostly due to French, Swiss and German entrepreneurs, attracted by the presence of flourishing natural resources and of a railway connecting the Po Valley with the Western part of Europe. This is why such transnational entrepreneurs established the first industrial textile plants in the towns of Borgone, Chianocco, Sant'Ambrogio and Sant'Antonino. In addition to the textile sector, the metallurgical (Buttigliera Alta), the chemical (Susa, Avigliana) and the electrical (Alpignano) business sectors started their initial investment during that period. Similarly, the upper valley experienced a significant economic development only from the 1930s, when the construction of the first ski resort in Sestriere favored a gradual process of conversion of the historical agro-forestry-pastoral vocation to a new economy based on winter tourism (Aime, 2016). Today, the upper valley continues to be identified as the territory that hosted the 2006 Winter Olympic Games, while the lower valley cannot be described unequivocally. In geographic studies, the lower valley constitutes a sort of archetypal intermediate space, namely a place that cannot be clearly defined for its intrinsic characteristics (Sutton, 2013). As such, Blanchard (1943) was one of the first that identified the existence of two main different territorial systems in the Alpine valleys. Further studies introduced the importance of using socio-economic criteria (Veyret & Veyret, 1967) to classify the upper and lower valleys. Unfortunately, for many years, the lower valley has been described, using a metro-centric perspective, as an appendix of the most urbanized areas. Adopting such a narrow viewpoint, most studies have put little attention on the fundamental role played by the presence of a unique set of intrinsic resources and dynamics of the lower valley (Sutton, 2011). Neglecting the presence of an interconnected net of multiple features within the spatial planning (Sutton, 2011; Ferlaino & Rota, 2013), that literature has often contributed in generating conflictual outcomes *in understanding and classifying the intrinsic characteristics (orographic, social and economical) of low valleys.* For instance, the No TAV movement has seen the presence of a dichotomy between the different needs of those living in the upper and in the lower part of the valley. It is also important to underline the existence of a "middle" valley[3] (IRES, 2019; Barbera et al., 2018), a territorial *"connector"* between the tourist district and the metro-mountain area of the lower valley, characterized by the presence of a rich PDO (Protected Designation Origin) and DOCG[4] wine and food production.

From an opposite and complementary viewpoint, the Susa Valley is located in the middle of a vast European region, the macro-region of the Western Alps, which had its own formal expression in the COTRAO[5] and which is in contact with the major axes of European development. Secondly, the Susa Valley can be considered as the southern periphery of the Lotharingia and part of the Mediterranean corridor. To contextualize and describe its centrality within the European macro-region it is worth referring to the multiform and extensive concept of *corridor* (Garavaglia, 2017), understood as a *"space in which the flows (of people, goods, information) become denser and assume particular importance in defining the characteristics of the social and economic*

---

[3] For the taxonomic proposal of the Susa Valley, we referred to several different contributions including: Aime (2016); Barbera et al. (2018); IRES (2017); IRES (2019); Ferlaino et al. (2019); Garavaglia (2017).

[4] *Label guaranteeing the quality and origin of a wine* and agricultural production.

[5] COTRAO (Communauté de travail des Alpes Occidentales) was an association of regions, formed in 1982, which includes Liguria, Piedmont, Valle d'Aosta, Rhône Alpes, Provence-Alpes-Côte-d'Azur and the cantons of Geneva, Valais and Vaud.

context" (Garavaglia, 2017, p. 1740). The polysemic concept of corridor, although still not well defined (Pain, 2011), is therefore useful to accompany the scientific, institutional and political debate on some relevant issues that intersect at the same time infrastructural (road, rail), environmental (ecological corridors), ICT (broadband networks) and urban aspects. In this view, the Susa Valley is placed in the middle of the European corridor for sustainable transportation, connecting east and west Europe. Establishing a corridor means to deeply impact on the economic and urban growth (see the discussion in Chapter 6 about the history of the Turin-Lyon megaproject), but also, on the typologies of endemic social issues, that should be included in proper planning spaces for post-metropolitan development processes.[6]

Figure 1. Piedmont's valleys in dark gray and the research area including the Susa valley (1), the Sangone valley (2) and part of Chisone and Germanasca valleys (3)

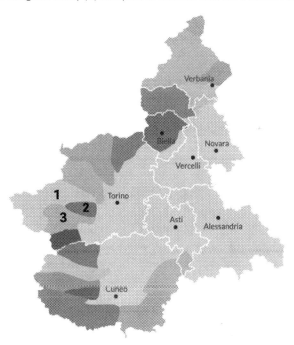

Source: authors' own elaboration adapted from https://hikerspiemonte.it/mappa/.

The Susa Valley is therefore a complex and multiform territory. In this study, our research area is represented by the local production system

---

[6] See for instance the discussion about the concept of "infrastructural territorialization" in Chapter 1 and the example of the Uganda railway.

(LPS) comprising 48 mountain municipalities belonging to the Susa Valley, and to same neighboring valleys such as Chisone, Germanasca, Sangone, Cenischia as they characterize a unique area with common structural and cultural features (Barbera et al., 2018).

7.2.3. A new institutional perspective to overcome the "marginality" of places

As mentioned in the previous paragraph, in the last decade the theme of mountain areas has gained visibility and a new, unprecedented centrality in the academic and institutional debate. In general, there has been an overcoming of the rhetorical and traditional image of the mountain as a bucolic place of Sunday *loisir* that has opened the doors to a representative dimension of the mountain as a place of social and economic innovation (Barbera et al., 2019; Barbera & De Rossi, 2021). Traditionally, the phenomenon of the discovery of the mountain and human settlement in the highlands has been interpreted in a multiform and not unique way: a "*traditional*" vision that conveys the image, in some respects romantic, of the mountain as an uncontaminated place to be preserved, and a new "*urban-centric*", playful-recreational image according to which the highlands are "*dépendances*" of the city and of its consumerist "*use*" (Dematteis, 2016). Against this approach, today we need a potential and new convergence of interests and actions between mountain and city/plain, with a view towards the geographical, operational and cultural proximity, the mutual benefits and the potential for a place-based innovation that draws from "diversity" of natural and cultural "places" (Becattini, 2015). As previously mentioned, the ultimate objective of the Italian National Strategy for Inland Areas (SNAI) is to reduce the socio-economic inequalities of the territories, in order to prevent the increase in differences and trigger socio-territorial mechanisms of "revenge" of the places left behind. Such places can be described as those marginalized areas that could harbor anger and resentment, which often translates into political support for populist forces (Rodriguez-Pose, 2018). In this regard, although we will not deal specifically with the issue of the No TAV protest, the results of our qualitative research confirm what has already been highlighted by other studies about the reasons for local resentment resulting from a lack of local/supra-local consultation and concerted dialogue between local communities and institutional actors, which has fuelled for three decades the conflict and the No TAV movement (Giliberto & Giudice, 2005; Bobbio & Dansero, 2008; Grisoni, 2015; Garavaglia, 2017; Della Porta & Piazza, 2008).

The one against the construction of the Turin-Lyon HSR in the Susa Valley is a very significant case of mobilization against the realization of a large infrastructure that has become well visible and highly discussed in Italy and Europe (*see* Chapter 6). The inhabitants, mobilized in committees and associations, together with social centers and environmental groups, had conceived their action as a defense of common goods and principles of universal value. They did not simply say no[7] to the megaproject, but also somehow developed alternative proposals from a political, social and entrepreneurial viewpoint (Della Porta & Piazza, 2008). A fundamental step in the construction of this long-standing conflict was the (re)definition of the identity of the protestors: the No TAV struggle rested on a development of the local identity that draws on a past of vivid partisan Resistance during the Second World War, in which the call, real or symbolic, to the Resistance and to the resistant "temperament" of the locals is omnipresent. The environmental, social and no-global issues on which the protest was built are undeniably linked to the common perception of a "denied" identity. Indeed, some studies (Della Porta & Piazza, 2008) highlight how the protagonists of the No TAV fight insist on an identitarian fracture, as a result of their incomplete and denied historical, socio-economic path: the anticipated process of industrialization of the lower valley characterized, from the post-war period onwards, a working and industrialized valley inhabited by "quasi-mountaineers", people who worked in factories in the lower valley or near Turin.[8] The subsequent process of de-industrialization of the valley, since the 1970s, weakened the working, industrial and urban character of the people of the valley, making way for an identity that was no longer urban-industrial or mountainous. These identitarian perceptions and the claims made by No TAV are partly intertwined with the demands and the lifestyle of the so-called "new mountaineers", which will be dealt with in section 7.4.

7.3. Methodology

The qualitative research allowed us to identify and analyze the conditions that supported forms of entrepreneurship in the Susa Valley, shedding light on the relationships and aspects that favored business, as well as the critical issues that hindered the establishment and development of new entrepreneurial activities.

---

[7] Indeed, the No TAV movement cannot be simply classified as a NIMBY (Not In My Back Yard) social movement.

[8] Turin is the provincial capital as well as the largest city near the valley.

The selection criteria of the sample of interviewees followed both the representativeness of the entrepreneurial and institutional population of the Susa Valley, and the accessibility of the interviewed subjects. Specifically, on the business population of 11,459 companies operating in the 48 municipalities identified as the research area, 2 groups of 20 enterprises were originally selected, distinguishing between medium-large and micro-small firms.[9] The sample originally conceived was re-selected, given the impossibility or lack of willingness of some company managers to be interviewed. The final sample consisted of 13 micro and small enterprises, 10 large enterprises, 8 Mayors of the Susa valley and 12 key institutional actors, 4 associations and/or third sector entities, in order to depict the local ecosystem (Pichierri, 2001; Camoletto & Bellandi, 2021).

The semi-structured interviews focused in particular on: the Alpine infrastructure, the innovative entrepreneurial, social and environmental projects implemented in the Susa Valley in the last five years, local identity, the Turin-Lyon HSR case and the metro-mountain connections. Table 1 shows the list of interviewees grouped by typologies. The semi-structured interviews were made mostly in 2021 during the Covid-19 pandemic, conducted for the most part online, and lasting about an hour and a half on average. The interviews were then transcribed and analyzed according to the Constant Comparative Method (Boeije, 2002). The numbers shown in the table are then used as a reference throughout the whole discussion.

Table 1. Interviewees

Type	Interviewees
Mayors	26, 29, 31, 32, 33, 34, 38, 39
Local institutions and authorities	7, 8, 9, 13, 16, 21, 24, 25, 27, 28, 30, 36, 40
Farmers/owner of agricultural activity	1, 2, 3, 4, 5, 6, 10, 14, 18, 19, 20
Commercial activity (third sector)	11, 17
Big companies	22, 23, 41, 42, 43, 44, 45, 46, 47
Cooperative/local association	12, 15, 35, 37

Source: authors' own elaboration.

---

[9] Our original sample consisted of 2 macro-groups of 40 medium-large and 40 micro-small enterprises. Out of 80 subjects contacted, only 25 agreed to be interviewed.

7.4. Results and findings

The research allowed to deepen what previous studies had highlighted about the new forms of entrepreneurship and neo-ruralism that have arisen more and more consistently in the Alps in the last decade (Corrado et al., 2014; Barbera et al., 2019). Alongside the emergence of a new paradigm of relationality (Sacco et al., 2006), the increasing spread of reciprocity practices in the third sector (Fazzi, 2016) - which has in part led to the overcoming of traditional contrasting socio-economic paradigms (reciprocity vs exchange - axiological individualism vs axiological holism, *Cfr.* Zamagni, 2007, 2007a) - and the birth and development of new economic models in which relational goods acquire increasing importance (Frey & Stutzer, 2010), we have seen the emergence of new forms of entrepreneurship. Such forms are driven by motivations different from those traditionally considered among the main Schumpter's pushes (Sacco et al., 2006) to entrepreneurial action, including the will and thirst for power, the desire for success and the pleasure of realization (Swedberg, 1998). The phenomenon of the *"return to the mountain"* is part of these new entrepreneurial experiences and it is interesting, in the eyes of social scientists and policy makers, for at least two interconnected reasons: on the one hand, it allows to investigate from a geographical viewpoint the question of local development of the suburbs, with the aim of operationally and institutionally re-centralizing the territories on the margin; on the other hand, it draws attention to new forms of neo-rural entrepreneurship, often innovative and still hidden (Barbera & Parisi, 2019) which, while at present consist mostly of spontaneous and unplanned experiences, could be the starting point for a more coordinated, restocking process within local and supra-local spatial planning (that the SNAI aims to achieve). Moreover, the interviews highlight how, very often, these new forms of neo-ruralism intersect with innovative entrepreneurial proposals, outlining the profile of innovative entrepreneurs who give rise to phenomena of self-organization "bottom-up" in traditional areas of social innovation such as welfare and social integration, the rehabilitation of peripheral areas, health-care services and sustainable tourism.

Most of the small entrepreneurs interviewed launched new entrepreneurial initiatives in the last decade, especially in the agricultural sector (2, 3, 4, 6, 14, 19, 20) activating, in many cases, processes of productive diversification and multifunctionality. Such processes concern, alongside the cultivation of typical local products, recreational activities, accommodation and tourism activities (4, 14), training courses and educational programs

(4) about social inclusion [10] (6). In most cases, the interviews shed light on a life and entrepreneurial path *"aware"*, *"looking for a healthier lifestyle"*, in contact with nature and *"away from the stress of the city"*,[11] even though most of them often did not have previous work experience in agriculture or tourism (2, 3, 4, 6, 20). It is precisely this group of new rural entrepreneurs that conceived and implemented a diversified and multifunctional business project that normally combines agricultural activity in the processing of agricultural products and the sale of derivatives. This group also presents the highest levels of education [12] and shows a greater propensity for collaboration with colleagues, institutions and local companies (2, 3, 4, 20).

No less significant is the work of local associations and companies of the third sector, normally engaged in activities of cultural promotion (27, 28), the recovery of agricultural tradition and local seeds (16, 12) and services related to the mountain and metro-mountain development (40). In particular, a cooperative (40) operates to integrate people who come from outside and want to belong to the mountain lifestyle *"in the right way"*. To achieve this, the cooperative proposes customized solutions to satisfy the needs of those who have an entrepreneurial idea to implement in mountain areas but are *"urban citizens"*. The main aim of the cooperative is therefore to act as a *"mediator between the two worlds"*, activating *"mountain and metro-mountain connections"* and enhancing the role of the mountain territory as a *"privileged laboratory to create a new model of life"*, by highlighting *"its complexity and the cultural and operational micro-cosmos that characterize it"*. However, these complexity and cultural richness might not be sufficiently valued, for a number of interconnected reasons including: 1. the desertification of mountain areas, 2. the lack of adequate links with urban areas, 3. the shortage of educational, digital infrastructure and hospitals.

An interviewee (14), owner of a farm in Giaglione, attributes to the middle valley *"the same Franco-Provençal identity"*, characterized by a language still spoken among the locals, and by specific rituals and ceremonies that are repeated annually (including, the ceremony of the *Spadonari* and the *Bran*) and an *"agricultural and wine production"* that specifically concerns the municipalities of Novalesa, Venaus, Giaglione, Mattie, Meana. The interviewee points out that most of the municipalities of the middle *"Franco-Provençal"*

---

[10] Personal psychological paths and pet therapy.

[11] Most of the respondents emphasize the decision to move away from previous experiences of urban life and work that they considered no more satisfactory.

[12] 5 of the new entrepreneurs have a degree, 2 a high school diploma. Among other things, this data confirms what has been highlighted in Barbera & Parisi (2019) on the high cultural capital of social innovators.

valley are excluded from the local railway network, which led to "*a very strong depopulation*" since the Second post-war.

Regarding the *Occitan* municipalities of the upper valley, another interviewee (7) specifies how these municipalities match the former territory of the *Escartons* of Oulx and Pragelato: "*the Forest Consortium was born in 1953 with the aim of keeping alive the 'democratic culture' of the Escartons and with the task of managing the agro-forestry-pastoral heritage of the Susa Valley. In general, the actions of protection of the historical memory of the 'Republic' of the Escartons are intertwined with those of preservation and dissemination of the Occitan culture, prevalent in the municipalities of the upper valley*". [13] These interviewees (14, 7) question the state of the infrastructure and local services, highlighting the shortcomings of the hospital service, especially in the upper valley, where many inhabitants often turn to the French hospitals of Briançon or Saint-Jean de Maurienne, instead of going to the nearest hospital in Susa, which has been reduced "*to the level of a common first aid*" over time (7).

Interviewee 7 ascribes the phenomena of demographic decrease and the entrepreneurial impoverishment that occurred mainly since the second post-war to the lack of a political voice (and the non-representativeness of the electoral colleges of the upper valley). This matches the desertification in school and the consequent centralization in very few municipalities. Nevertheless, the problem of school desertification mainly concerns the middle and the upper valleys, whereas in the lower valley there are schools "*of excellent quality*" (36), such as the High School of Susa, and those of Avigliana and Giaveno. Farmers, in addition to highlighting the excessive complexity of administrative and managerial requirements and bureaucratic demands (3, 4, 10), which are often too expensive and complex for a holder of a micro and small business, raise the problem of local rail links

---

[13] The maintenance of the Occitan language in the Alpine valleys is attributable, in part, to the experience of self-government that affected this territory between the fourteenth and eighteenth centuries and which helped to preserve different cultural and linguistic aspects. The so-called "Republic of the Escartons" was born in 1343 in reaction to the feudal claims of the castellan of Briançon, in order to defend the common local interests. The federation of Escartons enjoyed administrative, tax and military autonomy, as well as providing for the free movement of goods, characterizing a very rich and socially-advanced territory (interviewee 30, for example, recalls how already in the fourteenth century women could dispose of their property); that is the reason why this federation is normally called "Republic". In 1713, with the Treaty of Utrecht, France gave up the Escartons of Casteldelfino, Oulx and Pragelato to the Savoy Crown. Progressively, with the French Revolution and the subsequent Restoration, the "democratic" rights which characterized the Federation were progressively eroded by the Savoy administration.

and, in general, the shortcomings of the local transport system (buses and shuttles for inter-municipal and Turin connections). Some municipalities in the middle valley are even excluded from the rail link (14); moreover, many respondents in the lower valley describe the transport system as too *"Turin-centric and unable to adequately connect the urban metropolis to the mountain"* (16).

Also a local institution official dwells on the transport deficiencies, deepening the argument in the direction of a potential metro-mountain connection: *"It is not a question of which service is lacking. It is rather disturbing that the Alpine areas are always considered marginal. The resources of the mountain serve the city but nothing is returned in economic and social terms to the mountain [...]. This perspective must be changed: until now politicians have reasoned in terms of 'what the mountain can do for the city', and, just recently, 'what the city can do for the mountains' [...]. The one-fits-all perspective is no longer possible: every territory has its own necessities and needs its services and it is not correct to always focus on urban areas. Moreover, the concept of 'marginal areas' or 'disadvantaged areas' is wrong in itself"* (21).

35 out of 47 respondents stress the importance of strengthening the networks of collaboration with the city through an improvement of the local transport system, which should connect the municipalities of the valley with the town. Only one interviewee questioned the possibility of integrating the urban lifestyle and the mountain identity, underlining that the needs and priorities are completely different (32). In general, however, interviewees hope for a greater connection with urban areas to be achieved through the strengthening of the local rail network and the digital infrastructure, but not only: some respondents emphasize how, to get to a fruitful metro-mountain connection, a change of perspective in the management of metro-mountain interdependencies and a more balanced and less *"Turin-centric"* vision is necessary:

> *"Of course I do. The only thing I can't stand is being administered with a Turin-centric vision [...]"* (7);
> *"I believe and hope so. Unfortunately the mountain was seen as a playing field where all the powerful lobbies (from skiing, hunting, to water management) made money..."* (39).

Almost everyone emphasizes the importance of the protection and good governance of the mountains, primarily through a wise management of the territory, but also from the point of view of institutional representation and local politics. This should be done even before the management of possible and desirable connections between the city and the mountain.

The qualitative research has therefore highlighted the presence of a local ecosystem that shares common resources and specific local identities. Moreover, it has shed light on the complexity, in sociological, geographic and economic terms, of mountain territories, namely:

1. the orographic, social and economic variety that characterizes the different mountain territories and valleys;
2. the issue of the return to the mountain connected to the work and life experience of the new mountaineers;
3. the related issue of the need, expressed by the respondents, for the environmental protection and the conservation of the Alpine ecosystem;
4. the lack of a political voice and institutional representation of mountain communities;
5. the lack of appropriate schools, hospitals, transports and digital infrastructure in the Alpine territory of the Susa Valley;
6. the desirable connection between the two worlds, the mountain and the city, by fostering an advocated "*metro-mountain*" connection;
7. the existence of a mountain identity (see section 7.4.1.), real or perceived, that feeds on different historical paths and identitarian perceptions (e.g. the "Occitan" and "Franco-Provençal" identities), connected both to the experiences of the No TAV struggle and of new mountaineers.

There is no doubt that the lack of infrastructure, services and the little attention paid to cultural and productive diversity of the mountain environment, has only partially activated a shared awareness about the importance of an advocated metro-mountain connection, by encouraging original local development paths that would draw simultaneously from urban and mountain resources. This is in spite of the increasing attractiveness of mountain areas and the Susa Valley, in which novel entrepreneurial paths have been launched in the last decade (very often by former "urban" entrepreneurs) and that are intertwined with the demands and perspectives advocated by SNAI at the national level.

7.4.1. A "responsible" ecosystem with a strong identity

Referring to the academic and institutional literature (European Commission, 2001, 2011; Dalshrud, 2008), we define "responsible" companies as those that aim to integrate on a voluntary basis the social, environmental, and governance issues of their stakeholders in their corporate mission or the business strategies they implement. To this end, they should take into account an internal dimension of Corporate Social Responsibility (addressed to internal stakeholders such as employees) and an external dimension (aimed primarily at external stakeholders such as local and supra-local communities). In the same way, to define and identify "innovative" good practices implemented by public and private entities, we refer to the concept, albeit broad and undefined, of *social innovation* to indicate new solutions to social problems and needs for which a response has not yet been found through traditional intervention and which, at the same time, stands for a more effective, sustainable or fair approach (Murray et al., 2010).

On the CSR side, only large companies have implemented significant corporate welfare policies. In particular, the human resources manager of a local company (23) tells: "*We are a company born in the valley in 1954, and that has always tried to employ the people of the valley. We have about 900 employees, mostly women: it is our choice, because we think they are more accurate than men. We are a S.p.A.,*[14] *but one of our main goals is to be at the service and cooperate with workers, as it was in the initial project and in the founder's dream [...]. We have almost no turnover, because we've always tried to put our workers at ease and do not consider them numbers. Among the many welfare measures implemented, we provide free assistance for pension practices and we also provide workers with health care assistance. Basically, we have always implemented welfare measures since the beginning [...]. We have always been very close to those who get sick, and we meet their needs from the point of view of the work-life balance [...], especially mothers. We aim at creating a peaceful workplace*".

But there are also original and innovative initiatives implemented by the owners of agricultural, individual or family-run micro-enterprises, which reveal a greater dynamism in terms of environmental and social sustainability. For instance, an interviewee (4), head of a multi-functional farm in Mattie founded in 2000, has gradually transformed and diversified its business, originally born as a tourist refuge for mountain bikes. This entrepreneur decided to enrich the initial entrepreneurial project with catering and agricultural activities related to the cultivation of fruits and medicinal herbs, and the production and sale of derivatives such as essential oils and creams, as well as also activating since 2020 a collaboration with a cooperative in Burkina Faso for the collection and processing of shea nuts. A psychotherapist from Turin and founder of a social farm in the lower valley (6) combined the agricultural activity with social activities of recovery of children and weak subjects through psychotherapeutic paths and pet therapy. Interviewee 14, a primary school teacher, since 1997 has completely devoted herself to the family-run farm: in over twenty years of agricultural work

---

[14] A stock company.

and promotion of her local wines' production, she obtained a quality certification for the Avanà Bequet grape variety and has recently launched new sustainable production processes for local wines, potatoes and vegetables.

More generally, all respondents, both entrepreneurs and institutional subjects, stress the need to protect the Alpine territory and revitalize it by promoting initiatives that bring to light local specificities that combine environmental protection issues, social cohesion and tourism promotion. Among the most significant initiatives in this area, it is worth highlighting the Mill of Bruzolo where *"young boys and girls have recently renovated the structure of the ancient stone mill, creating a short chain of cultivation of local grains, above all ancient grains, with the collaboration of local farmers to then process the flour and resell the derived products inside the same mill"* (1); or the *CanapaValleSusa* association, founded in 2014, which brought together a number of growers with the idea of cultivating local hemp and helping its members with training and entrepreneurial projects related to the transformation of hemp in food, textile and therapeutic products (1); then, the activities of the Forest Consortium, that include the creation of a wood chip branch for energy consumption in the 14 municipalities of the upper valley; the activities of Con.I.S.A. (the Social care Consortium of the Susa Valley and Val Sangone), especially in the field of immigration management, and finally the cultural valorisation plan implemented by the association *Valle di Susa, Tesori e Arte di Cultura Alpina* since 2003. There are also more specific and smaller initiatives such as the MedicalBus service, an assistance and first aid service in small villages that are far from health centers; the project *Salviamo Il Cibo*, supervised by the municipality of Susa, for the recovery of food surpluses, activated in collaboration with the ASL (Local Health Authority), Italian Red Cross (CRI), CARITAS, the Scout Group of Susa; the *MigrAlp* project (2017) that aims at hosting migrants and helping them crossing the Alps to reach France, realized in partnership with some third sector companies and with the active involvement of border municipalities (Bardonecchia, Oulx, Claviere), the Italian Red Cross and the *Rainbow for Africa* association.

The relevance of a responsible economic action combined with environmental protection demands is generally ascribed to a specific *"mountain"* identity, positively[15] described and defined as *"rustic"*, *"communitari-*

---

[15] Some questions were aimed at investigating identitarian perceptions of the respondents and their operational link with the town. One of the questions was as follows: *"The academic and institutional literature considers it important to develop a connection between the town and the mountain (a "metro-mountain" connection): the city can for instance provide entrepreneurial resources, contribution in demographic terms; the mountain provides environmental resources and clean energy sources. What is your relationship*

an", "*genuine*" (4); "*welcoming*" and "*tireless*" (5); "*supportive*", "*sharing*", "*fair*", "*proud*", "*stubborn*" (9); "*determined*" (14); "*aware*" (21); "*tenacious*" and "*reliable*" (23); "*hospitable*" and "*simple*" (37). Only in two cases, the mountain identity is described by interviewees in terms of "*lack of resourcefulness*", "*nostalgia for the past*", "*resignation*" and "*mental closure*". This identity perception, as one interviewee states (1), is even more marked in the case of the new mountaineers who moved to the mountains to embrace a lifestyle more in line with their needs.

> "*We are urban citizens who moved to the mountains after university. Let' s say that we lived in the city and we chose to leave it for the mountain [...]. After my father-in-law retired, we decided to take over the business, choosing to create an alternative lifestyle [...]. Over the years, we have developed a hatred towards the city: I believe that the urban agglomeration and the urban lifestyle are a bit parasitic with respect to the environmental resources of the world [...]. I realize that the city also offers many opportunities in terms of cultural and recreational space, which are lacking here in the mountains. However, the mountain does not need the city nor the tourists [...]. I have greatly negativized the urban reality and so I don't see how it can connect to the mountain*" (1).

In its most radical forms, the three-fold responsible/sustainable-innovative-mountain identity has resulted in some initiatives such as Etinomìa, considered as a unique experience by most of the respondents. Indeed, a previous research about the identity dynamics of the No TAV movement in the Susa Valley (Soubirou, 2018) identifies the birth of the protest and the movement as the basis of a new local economic paradigm based on solidarity, an economy defined through a set of activities of production, exchange and consumption that aimed at the democratization of the economy through civic engagement (Fraisse et al., 2007), and in which the values of social justice, environmental protection, territorial identity and cultural diversity (Laville, 2014) became the hallmarks of a strongly territorialized community of which Etinomia was the spokesman.[16] "*Born in the hot period of the construction of*

---

with the city? Do you feel part of a territory that is part of the city? Would you like to feel part of the city or strengthen connections with the city?".

40 respondents out of 47 describe their identity as a "mountain" identity.

[16] The empirical analysis carried out through a series of qualitative interviews highlights the presence of a Valsusa society of the lower valley, the heart of the No TAV movement, and a small entrepreneurial ecosystem connected to some fundamental institutional bodies (such as Etinomìa) which is identified in the values of: 1) adherence to the movement No TAV, 2) territoriality understood as the centrality of the local dimension of the movement; 3) autonomy, self-government and opposition to any kind of al-

the Turin-Lyon HSR, when several entrepreneurs came together to show that the work was for progress and we instead, as a group of entrepreneurs, we wanted to show that there could be an ethical economy where money comes after environmental protection. Respect, tolerance and ethics are the basis of our association policy" (24). Once again, even in the most extreme and radicalized forms, the principles of sustainability, innovation and territorial identity underpin an innovative and sustainable local action.

To conclude, in most cases, the interviewees (especially farmers and small entrepreneurs) reveal a proud mountain identity that strives for environment and local community protection. In some cases, this identity can be seen as hostile or, at least, cautious in highlighting the benefits that would derive from the realization of the Lyon-Turin HSR. As highlighted by interviews and some academic literature (Della Porta & Piazza, 2008), the reasons for the No TAV protests that arose in the early 1990s, came precisely from the lack of an inclusive, transparent and open governance that drove the realization of the megaproject, i.e. the lack of an advocated *institutional sustainability,* a real dialogic approach, involving all the stakeholders, and that takes into account also the needs and the views of the local community.

7.5. Conclusions

This study has provided an opportunity for a cross-disciplinary investigation and for the deepening of several themes, strands of research and debates that characterize the mountain matter, the metro-mountain connection, and the importance of considering territorial identity when conceiving and implementing a megaproject. Specifically, the Susa Valley was a privileged investigation laboratory for at least four reasons:

1. this case highlighted the complexity of the mountain issue. In the past, policy makers referred very often to the mountain territory with a one-way perspective that did not take into account historical-anthropological, socio-economic and production differences that distinguish the different valleys and mountain territories;
2. the analysis provided an initial starting point for a deeper investigation of individual and collective identities in the Susa Valley, highlighting how the mountain issue is not linked exclusively to orographic factors but primarily to real and perceived work-life relationships, community perceptions and complex feelings on the sense of belonging;

---

ienation; 4) friendliness, respect and mutual goodwill; 5) mutual relations; 6) solidarity and care for the weakest; 7) continuity of local action as a temporal continuum between past, present and future (Soubirou, 2018, p. 94).

3. the interviews shed light on some life and work experiences attributable to the so-called "new mountaineers", experiences that are numerically circumscribed but qualitatively relevant to overcome the concepts of extractivism, patrimonialism and romanticization, and consider and embed the concepts of innovation, dynamism and complexity when dealing with the mountain issue;
4. the mountain identity, declared by most of the interviewees, is strongly linked to criteria of social and environmental sustainability. In this sense, the process of *infrastructural territorialization*, although the Turin-Lyon HSR megaproject is yet to be completed, has strengthened over time the local identity, characterized by strong environmental and social values. The protection of the mountain landscape and the local cultural heritage plays a primary role among all opponents. The three decade-long No TAV protest proved how every phase of a megaproject, from the planning to the construction or the operation phase, needs a sustainable management from an economic, social, environmental and institutional viewpoint. This should be supported by a dialogic accounting approach, to include all affected and involved stakeholders through a democratic and inclusive stakeholder management process (See Chapter 1 and 2 of this book for an introductory and general discussion). Megaprojects in general, indeed, involve a vast array of stakeholders who often lack, as in this case, an adequate representation and political/institutional voice in decision-making processes. Moreover, the management of a megaproject must be in line with the Sustainable Development Goals (SDGs), where nature and the natural environment, the respect of local communities and identities must be necessarily taken into account. Hence, our research highlighted some important issues:

– a general awareness, and sometimes resentment, by institutional actors and small entrepreneurs about the shortage of certain services and the lack of infrastructure (transport, schools, hospitals...) that would inhibit a true local mountain development;
– a shared consciousness that we are still far from considering the mountain a not negligible place of socio-economic development, which is also linked to the lack of a local, political voice and an adequate institutional representation;
– the interviewees' perception about the difficulty of an advocated operational connection between the mountain and the city, which would give rise to a real metro-mountain development;
– the exclusion of mountain communities from important decision-making processes that has led to a strengthening of a *"mountain"* identity described as *"communitarian"*, *"genuine"*, *"welcoming"*,

"*tireless*", "*supportive*", "*sharing*", "*fair*", "*proud*", "*stubborn*", "*determined*", "*aware*", "*tenacious*" and "*reliable*", "*hospitable*" and "*simple*". These statements convey the aforementioned values of sustainability and social fairness.

Finally, although further research is needed in other mountain contexts, this study dwelt on the operational and theoretical link connecting the concepts of sustainability-responsibility/social innovation/neo-ruralism and metro-mountain experiences that today characterize the phenomena of innovative entrepreneurship in the Susa Valley. Future research may probably reinforce this hypothesis, investigating the metro-mountain development in other areas in light of the concepts of geographical and urban proximity, sustainability, corporate social responsibility and social innovation. Moreover, this research shed light on the importance of the local community's role in shaping/re-shaping a local territorial identity that can be in line or contrast with exogenous phenomena.

7.6. Summary

This chapter has introduced the main topics of neo-rural entrepreneurship, relying on the debate about the new "centrality" of the mountain areas, traditionally conceived as intermediate or marginal territories. In particular, the analysis of the Susa Valley in the Alpine Valley allows us to explore different intertwined research topics: 1. the forms of neo-ruralism that characterize the life and work experience of new "entrepreneurs-mountaineers"; 2. the local identity, characterized by strong social and environmental values, 3. the case of the Turin-Lyon HSR megaproject, 4. the metro-mountain connections. These different topics allow exploring the phenomenon of metro-mountain development in light of the concepts of geographical and cultural proximity (connecting the mountain to urban contexts), sustainability, Corporate Social Responsibility and social innovation.

References

Aime, M. (2016). *Fuori dal tunnel: viaggio antropologico nella val di Susa*. Mimesis.

Bagnasco, A. (1977). *Tre Italie. La problematica territoriale dello sviluppo italiano*. Il Mulino.

Balducci, A., Curci, F. & Fedeli, V. (2017). *Oltre la metropoli: l'urbanizzazione regionale in Italia. Oltre la metropoli*. Guerini e Associati. Kindle Edition.

Barbera, F., Miraglio, N., Pettenati, G. & Tipaldo, G. (2018). *Progetto IN.S.I.&M.E. L'altra Valle. Un progetto di sviluppo locale per le piccole imprese e il turismo in Valle di Susa*. Università degli Studi di Torino.

Barbera, F. & Parisi, T. (2019). *Innovatori sociali. La sindrome di Prometeo nell'Italia che cambia*. Il Mulino.

Barbera, F., Di Monaco, R., Pilutti, S. & Sinibaldi, E. (2019). *Dall'alto in basso: Imprenditorialità diffusa nelle terre alte piemontesi*. Rosenberg & Sellier.

Barbera, F. & De Rossi, A. (2021). *Metromontagna: Un progetto per riabitare l'Italia*. Donzelli Editore.

Barca, F., McCann, P. & Rodríguez-Pose, A. (2012). The case for regional development intervention: place-based versus place-neutral approaches. *Journal of regional science, 52*(1), 134–152.

Becattini, G. (1978). The development of the light industry in Tuscany: An interpretation. *Economic Notes, 2*(3), 107–123.

Becattini, G. (1989). Riflessioni sul distretto industriale marshalliano come concetto socioeconomico. *Stato e Mercato*, 111–128.

Becattini, G. (Ed.). (2001). *Il caleidoscopio dello sviluppo locale: trasformazioni economiche nell'Italia contemporanea*. Vol. 2. Rosenberg & Sellier.

Becattini, G. (2015). *La coscienza dei luoghi: il territorio come soggetto corale*. Donzelli.

Blanchard, R. (1943). *Les Alpes occidentales*. Fayard.

Bobbio, L. & Dansero, E. (2008). *La TAV e la valle di Susa. Geografie in competizione*. Umberto Allemandi & C. Editore.

Boeije, H. (2002). A purposeful approach to the constant comparative method in the analysis of qualitative interviews. *Quality and quantity*, 36, 391–409.

Bondonio, P., Dansero, E. & Mela, A. (Eds.) (2006). *Olimpiadi, oltre il 2006. Torino 2006: secondo rapporto sui territori olimpici*. Carrocci.

Bonomi, A. (2013). *Il capitalismo in-finito. Indagini sui territori della crisi*. Einaudi.

Camoletto, S. & Bellandi, M. (2021). Forme di sviluppo locale «ibride»: il caso della provincia di Cuneo. *Stato e mercato, 41*(3), 389–420.

Cersosimo, D., Ferrara, A.R. & Nisticò, R. (2018). L'Italia dei pieni e dei vuoti. In De Rossi, A. (Ed.) (2018). *Riabitare l'Italia: le aree interne tra abbandoni e riconquiste*. Donzelli.

Corrado, F., Dematteis, G. & Di Gioia, A. (Eds.) (2014). *Nuovi montanari. Abitare le Alpi nel XXI secolo*. Vol. 31. Franco Angeli.

Dahlsrud, A. (2008). How corporate social responsibility is defined: an analysis of 37 definitions. *Corporate social responsibility and environmental management, 15*(1), 1–13.

Daverio, S. (2013). *Valle di Susa. Tesori di Arte e Cultura Alpina*. https://www.parchialpicozie.it/contents/project/PVT_protocollo_4.pdf, retrieved July 2023, 30.

Della Porta, D. & Piazza, G. (2008). *Le ragioni del no*. Feltrinelli.
Dematteis, G. (2016). La città ha bisogno della montagna. La montagna ha diritto alla città. *Scienze del territorio, 4*, 10–17.
De Rossi, A. (2018). *Riabitare l'Italia: le aree interne tra abbandoni e riconquiste*. Donzelli.
European Commission, Directorate-General for Employment (2001). *Promoting a European Framework for Corporate Social Responsibility: Green Paper*. Office for Official Publications of the European Communities.
European Commission (2011). *A renewed EU strategy 2011–14 for Corporate Social Responsibility*.
European Commission (2011a). *WHITE PAPER. Roadmap to a Single European Transport Area – Towards a competitive and resource efficient transport system*. https://eur-lex.europa.eu/, EN (europa.eu).
European Union (2013). Common Transport Policy. https://www.europarl.europa.eu/RegData/etudes/fiches_techniques/2013/050601/04A_FT(2013)050601_EN.pdf, retrieved July 2023, 30.
Fazzi, L. (2016). *Il servizio sociale nel terzo settore*. Maggioli.
Ferlaino, F. & Rota, F.S. (Eds.) (2013). *La montagna italiana. Confini, identità e politiche*. Franco Angeli.
Ferlaino, F., Rota, F.S. & Dematteis, G. (Eds.) (2019). *Le montagne del Piemonte*. IRES Piemonte.
Fraisse, L., Guérin, I. & Laville, J.L. (2007). Economie solidaire: des initiatives locales à l'action publique. Introduction. *Revue Tiers Monde, 2*, 245–253.
Frey, B.S. & Stutzer, A. (2010). Happiness and public choice. *Public Choice*, 144, 557–573.
Garavaglia, L. (2017). *Città dei flussi. I corridoi territoriali in Italia*. Vol. 4. goWare & Edizioni Guerini e Associati. Kindle Edition.
Giliberto, J. & Giudice, E. (Eds.) (2005). *NO TAV. Cronache di una valle incazzata*. NEOS Edizioni.
Grisoni, A. (2015). Conflictualité autour des marqueurs temporels: sociohistoire de 25 ans du mouvement Notav. *VertigO, 15*(2), 1–16.
IRES (2017). *PTR Regione Piemonte. Analisi di aggiornamento delle componenti strutturali e delle vocazioni degli AIT piemontesi*.
IRES (2019). *Le comunità dei vini DOC e DOCG della Città Metropolitana di Torino. Inquadramento territoriale e analisi dei valori condivisi*. ALCOTRA 2014-2020. Progetto n. 1540.
Laville, J.L. (2014). Postface. In Hersent, M. & Palma Torres, A. (Eds.) (2014). L'économie solidaire en pratiques. *Sociologie économique*, 225–240.
Lutz, V.C. (1958). Il processo di sviluppo in un sistema economico 'dualistico'. *Moneta e credito, 11*(44).
Membretti, A. (2021). Le popolazioni metromontane: relazioni, biografie,

bisogni. In Barbera, F. & De Rossi, A. (2021). *Metromontagna: Un progetto per riabitare l'Italia*. Donzelli. Kindle Edition, 2092–2473.

MIUR (2013). *Strategia nazionale per le Aree interne: definizione, obiettivi, strumenti e governance. Accordo di partenariato 2014–2020*. https://www.miur.gov.it/documents/20182/890263/strategia_nazionale_aree_interne.pdf/d10fc111-65c0-4acd-b253-63efae626b19, retrieved July 2023, 30.

Murray, R., Caulier-Grice, J. & Mulgan, G. (2010). *The open book of social innovation*. Vol. 24. Nesta.

Pain, K. (2011). 'New Worlds' for 'Old'? Twenty-First Century Gateways and Corridors: Reflections on a European Spatial Perspective. *International Journal of Urban and Regional Research*, 35(6), 1154–1174.

Pichierri, A. (2001). Concertazione e sviluppo locale. *Stato e Mercato*, 62(2), 237–266.

Rodríguez-Pose, A. (2018). The revenge of the places that don't matter (and what to do about it). *Cambridge journal of regions, economy and society*, 11(1), 189–209.

Sacco, P.L., Vanin, P. & Zamagni, S. (2006). The economics of human relationships. *Handbook of the economics of giving, altruism and reciprocity*, 1, 695–730.

Soubirou, M. (2018). The No TAV Entrepreneurs' Transition towards a Sustainable Solidarity Economy: Pragmatic Analysis of a Social Innovation Process. *Journal of Entrepreneurial and Organizational Diversity*, 7(1), 88–110.

Sutton, K. (2010). *Le Lyon-Turin dans le Val de Suse: un aménagement nommé malaise*. Paper presented at Identité, Qualité et Compétitivité territoriale colloque ASRDLF-AISRe. Held in Aosta.

Sutton, K. (2011). *Les Nouvelles Traversées Alpines. Entre cospatialité de systèmes nationaux et recherche d'inter spatialités, une géopolitique circulatoire*. Thèse de doctorat en géographie, Université de Savoie.

Sutton, K. (2013). Dal basso al piede. Verso una riconsiderazione delle basse valli alpine. In Ferlaino, F. & Rota, F.S. (Eds.). *La montagna italiana. Confini, identità e politiche*. Franco Angeli.

Trigilia, C. (2005). *Sviluppo locale: un progetto per l'Italia*. Laterza.

Swedberg, R. (1998). *Joseph A. Schumpeter: vita e opere*. Bollati Boringhieri.

Veyret, P. (1950). Comptes Rendus Critiques, Les Grandes Alpes Françaises du Sud. In *Blanchard (R.). Les Alpes Occidentales*. Tome V. Les Grandes Alpes françaises du Sud. *Revue de Géographie Alpine*, 39(3), 605–612.

Veyret, P. & Veyret, G. (1967). *Au cœur de l'Europe, les Alpes*. Flammarion.

Zamagni, S. (2007). *L'economia del bene comune*. Città nuova.

Zamagni, S. (2007a). Il bene comune nella società post-moderna. Proposte per l'azione politico-economica. *Rivista di studi politici*, 4, 85–122.

Chapter 8
CONCLUSION

> ABSTRACT: *What role does accounting play for the sustainable management of megaprojects? What major impacts can be associated with the development of a transnational megaproject on people, economies, and the natural environment? What systems can be implemented to accompany the development of infrastructure megaprojects toward greater transparency, openness, and inclusiveness? With the help of different methodologies, and through a specific business case, the answers to these questions begin to become apparent. And the insights we can glean can bring enriching benefits to theory and practice. Like all research work, this study has limitations and opportunities for future development. This and more will be discussed below.*
>
> SUMMARY: 8.1. A critique of the status quo. – 8.2. Limits and future opportunities. – 8.3. Summary. – *References*.

8.1. A critique of the status quo

In this book, the topic of megaproject development is of central importance, at least in terms of three different aspects of analysis: the sustainability of megaprojects, the impacts of megaprojects on the physical-natural and social environment, and the relationships in terms of the inclusiveness of stakeholders in megaproject construction decision-making process.

First, the book addresses how the sustainability of megaprojects is a complex issue that meets the definition of sustainable development not only within the word "development", but more articulately, megaprojects can hinder or facilitate the achievement of the Sustainable Development Goals. In fact, the critical analysis represented here is reinforced by several methodologies, from literature analysis to a specific coding of the SDGs mentioned in the sustainability reports of some of the world's major constructors. It is, therefore, appropriate to keep in mind that the transnational dimension of the megaprojects, as reported several times by the case examined, represents an additional layer of complexity, political, institutional, legal, and operational. An ecosystemic view of megaproject has been used in this book to introduce and claim the need for a more genuine approach towards Megaproject Social Responsibility.

Second, the book deals with what we refer to as impacts on the environment and society. Closely linked to the concept of sustainability, using an interdisciplinary perspective, the book presents the concept of impacts of megaprojects both with temporal and geographical characteristics (therefore the when and where), and with typological characteristics (the what, such as impacts on the natural and social environment), and finally, impacts towards stakeholders (who suffers and who can influence the creation of such impacts). Basing the analysis on the evolutions of stakeholder theory (Freeman & McVea, 2001), and on the application of these theories in the contexts of megaprojects (Wang et al., 2023), the book reinforces the international literature based on the critique of megaprojects as works whose strategic management is usually rich in technical errors, but also in programming and finance. The paradigm of infrastructural territorialization has been presented and used (Lesutis, 2021). Direct or indirect impacts are illustrated and discussed, also with reference to transnational projects, which thanks to the sociological perspective emerge in the example case, underlining how sometimes these projects are inserted in geographical contexts, which in turn are subject to important transformations (in the case illustrated here the context of metro-mountain is discussed in depth). The book gives us different perspectives, sometimes using opposing views, such as internal managers, site managers, and in opposition, industrialists from the areas involved and small entrepreneurs. In doing so, the purpose of the book is not absolutive, but a critique of the status quo, thus placing at the center of the discourse the involvement of the communities concerned in all the decision-making, strategic, and operational moments of the construction of a megaproject.

Third, stakeholders' inclusiveness. As derived from the second point of our analysis, the central focus of the book is on managing stakeholders' interests in relation to different decisions regarding megaprojects: policies (to do or not to do, and where to do); institutional (who is responsible and who executes); operational (how to do, with whom); management (is the management respecting budgets and plans? Are the impacts those estimated? Are negative impacts to be compensated, and how? Is it sufficient?). In all this discourse, often, stakeholders are marginalized to an often passive role, that is, to be simply informed of decisions. The historical legacy of tax-type infrastructure development policies, returns to be current for today's economies, as several strategic decisions will have to be taken in the future as a result of climate change. Therefore, even going through the concept of critical infrastructure, the book emphasizes that no decision is the right one, unless it is shared. Although the democratic nature of climate change affects us all, the impacts of climate change will not be democratic and will continue to be more costly and limiting, for those already fragile populations. Hence, when thinking about an infrastructure project, we must put people at the center. In this book, therefore, a "secular" and less dogmatic vision of stakeholders is proposed, which reflects the ecosystemic nature of the world. Both the perspectives of internal stakeholders (those who develop and execute a megaproject) and those who suffer the consequences (strong opponents, citizens, businesses) are included.

8.2. Limits and future opportunities

The main limitation of this research is due to the natural narrow-focus of the case study at hand, or rather, although the materiality of the study places the Turin-Lyon among the main European megaprojects, there are no comparisons with other megaprojects and the case analyzed. Despite this, the comparative strength, i.e. the international and in some ways transnational perspective, characterizes the volume in a transversal way. For example, in the historical perspective, where the main global infrastructure development corridors are presented (Chapter 1), in the benchmarking analysis, as illustrated in Chapter 3, and by the references to environmental justice contained within Chapter 5. Not only that, the specific characteristics of the Italian-French context and of the metro-mountain emerge in Chapter 7, and the perspective of transnational management in Chapter 6.

Finally, since international literature in the field of megaprojects is seen as an almost exclusive domain of scholars in the field of project management, in this book we advocate for an increasingly broader involvement of different disciplines, which can bring their own perspective of analysis. A wider collaboration between practitioners and academia is also of great interest, especially to shed light on some of the issues that characterize the current panorama in the field of sustainability, such as physical and chronic risks, those of transition related to climate change (especially in reference to the construction and end of life of major works), but also to the critical issues of modern slavery along the supply chain and the different levels of co-responsibility among suppliers and sub suppliers, contractors and subcontractors.

8.3. Summary

This book provides a comprehensive exploration of megaproject development, emphasizing its role in sustainable development, advocating for responsible and inclusive decision-making processes, and promoting collaboration across disciplines for addressing modern sustainability challenges.

References

Freeman, R.E. & McVea, J. (2001). A Stakeholder Approach to Strategic Management. In Hitt, M., Freeman, E. & Harrison, J. (Eds.) *The Blackwell Handbook of Strategic Management*. Blackwell Publishing.

Lesutis, G. (2021). Infrastructural territorialisations: Mega-infrastructures and the (re) making of Kenya. *Political Geography*, 90, 102459.

Wang, Z., He, Q., Locatelli, G., Wang, G. & Li, Y. (2023). Exploring Environmental Collaboration and Greenwashing in Construction Projects: Integrative Governance Framework. *Journal of Construction Engineering and Management*, 149(11), 04023109.

INDEX

Note: Locators in *italic* and **bold** refer to figures and tables; Locators followed by "n" refer to footnotes

B

Business2Nature: 22-27, 30

C

Critical Infrastructure: 2, **4**, 37-56, *42,* **44**
Commons: 91-97
Corporate Social Responsibility: 102, 120, 133, 134, 139

D

Dialogic Accounting: 15, 16, 132

E

Environmental Justice: 91-102
Environmentalism of the poor: 93-94

G

Governance: 4, 7, 13, 14, 37, **41,** 64, 69, 71, 72, **73,** 75, 77, 78, **79**, 105, 106, 116, 127, 128, 131

H

High-Speed Railway: 1, 2, 7, **44**, 57, 107-112

I

Infrastructural territorialization: 7, 10, 12, 63, 73, 97, 119, 132
Interview: 113-115, 128, **128**, 129-138
Iron law: **5**, 10-16

M

Megaproject Social Responsibility: 2, 21-24, 30, 48, 69, 76, **79**
Metro-mountain: 110, 123-126, 127, 130, 132

N

No TAV: 107-110, 116, 124, 126, 127, 133, 136-138

P

Project Management: 2, 3, 4, 5, 15, 21, 56, 57, 64, 68, 70, 71, **72**, 73, 75, **79,** 102

R

Resilience: 11, 14, 37, 39, **40,** 41, **42,** 43
Risk Management: **42, 70,** 69, 76

S

Social Innovation: 119, 120, 129, 134, 139
Social Network Analysis: 23, 25, 28, 29, 108, 113, 115, 116
Stakeholder Management: 1, 4, 5, 16, 22, 27, 69, 71, 73, 94, 98, 102, 103, 111, 132
Sublime: 9, 10, 12, 16
Susa: 2, 107, 109-112 119-142
Sustainable Development: 1, 2, **4-5**, 8, 10, 11, 12, 20, 21, 23, 26, 29, 35, 37, 38, 41, 47, 71, 116
Sustainable Development Goals: 11, 22, 23, 30, 35, 39, 40, 42-46, *46*, **47**, 47-49, 138
Sustainable Infrastructure: 1, 2, 4, **4**, **5**8-10, 13 -16, 43, 57-69, 71 8059, 60, 61, 63, *65*, 66, 67, *68*, 69, *70*, 78

T

TELT: 102, 103, 106, 107, 108, 109, 111, 112
TransEuropean Transport Network: 92, 103
Turin-Lyon HSR: 2, **5**, 42, 43, 96, 98, 99, 102, 103, 104, 106, 107, 111, 113, 114, 121, 122, 131, 132, 133

U

Uniqueness bias: 3, 9, 14, 16, 56

W

Wicked problem: 1, 2, 4